EPHESIANS

EPHESIANS

God's Plan for a
Thriving Church

Lewis Sperry Chafer

2024/01

Ephesians by Lewis Sperry Chafer.

Previously published as *The Epistle to the Ephesians.*
Originally published as *The Ephesian Letter.*

Published in 1991, 2024 by Kregel Classics, an imprint of Kregel
Publications, 2450 Oak Industrial Dr. NE, Grand Rapids, MI
49505.

Cataloging-in-Publication available at the Library of Congress.

ISBN 978-0-8254-4245-2

Printed in the United States of America

Contents

This book is affectionately dedicated to my brother, Rev. Rollin Thomas Chafer, D.D., whose life-long companionship, wise counsel, and tireless faithfulness in a great partnership service for God has gone far toward securing for it that measure of achievement which under divine favor has been wrought.

Publisher's Preface

Kregel Publications is happy to make available to a new reading audience this classic commentary on *The Epistle to the Ephesians*. First published in book form in 1935, these lectures originally appeared in *Revelation* magazine as a series of fifteen articles expounding the epistle, the apostle Paul's crucial letter to the church at Ephesus.

The first three chapters of the letter to the Ephesians contain doctrinal affirmations and the last three chapters are filled with practical exhortations, growing out of the truths expressed in the first half of the book. Calmly and deliberately, Paul writes to extol the person of Christ and explain the nature of the Church which is His body. He sees all believers as members of that body. The function of the Church is the revelation of a great mystery, a thing unrevealed in the Old Testament but unveiled after the resurrection of Christ. This mystery *is* the Church, not as an *organization* but as a living *organism* with Christ at its head. Paul explains this mystery in Ephesians 3:3 and 6.

A new generation of Bible students will find *The Epistle to the Ephesians* an understandable and deeply doctrinal exposition of this pivotal epistle.

THE PUBLISHERS

Preface

But for a slight revision in the text, the material presented in this volume was first published in the *Revelation* Magazine. The fifteen sections into which the book is divided correspond with the fifteen magazine articles and are published by the permission of the owners of *Revelation*.

No skeleton or outline of the Ephesian Letter is presented in this book other than that which is set forth in the *Contents*. The all-important features of the structure of the Ephesian Letter are, (1) The discovery of the precise message and character of the first division, Chapters 1-3, and (2) the logical relation which exists between the first division and that which follows.

Many books have been written on the Ephesian Letter. Some have been *exegetical* and some *devotional*. The distinctive aim of this treatment is *doctrinal*, and as this Letter has not been thus developed by writers generally it is hoped that the book may serve some worthwhile purpose and be, in some measure, "to the praise of the glory of his grace."

LEWIS SPERRY CHAFER

Dallas, Texas,
June 1, 1935

11

Section One

Ephesians 1:1, 2

1 Paul, an apostle of Jesus Christ by the will of God, to the saints which are at Ephesus, and to the faithful in Christ Jesus:

2 Grace be to you, and peace, from God our Father, and from the Lord Jesus Christ.

Unquestionably the greatest religious crisis in human history was experienced when, immediately following the death of Christ, the divine purpose was changed from the limitations of Judaism to the world-wide proclamation to Jew and Gentile alike of the infinite grace of God in and through Christ Jesus. The demand then was for a man who, under God, could receive the new divine revelation, formulate its doctrines, and contend for its claims. Saul of Tarsus was God's chosen instrument and to him were given two distinct revelations. The first was of the gospel of the saving grace of God through Christ, and is stated thus: "But I certify you, brethren, that the gospel which was preached of me is not after man. For I neither received it of man, neither was I taught it, but by the revelation of Jesus Christ" (Gal. 1:11, 12).

The second was of the divine age in the out-calling of the Church which, so far from being a continuation of any previous plan for Jew or Gentile, is said to be a mystery or sacred secret which was hid in past ages. This new purpose was not merely that a blessing was determined for Israel or for the Gentiles—each of which has a large place in unfulfilled prophecy—but rather that out from both Jews and Gentiles a new heavenly company was to be formed. The Scripture states, "For

13

this cause I Paul, the prisoner of Jesus Christ for you Gentiles, if ye have heard of the dispensation of the grace of God which is given me to you-ward; how that by revelation he made known unto me the mystery; . . . which in other ages was not made known unto the sons of men, as it is now revealed unto his holy apostles and prophets by the Spirit; that the Gentiles should be fellow-heirs, and of the same body, and partakers of his promise in Christ by the gospel" (Eph. 3:1-6). The Ephesian letter is a revelation of God's plan in and for the Church and is thus a development of the second revelation given to the Apostle Paul.

Date of the Epistle

By an abundance of evidence, we are assured that this Epistle was written A.D. 64 to the church at Ephesus by the Apostle Paul while in prison at Rome, and that it was closely associated with the letter to the Philippians and the letter to the Colossians. Probably all three letters were carried from Rome by Tychicus and noticeable, indeed, are the thirty-three similarities in the messages of the Ephesian and Colossian Epistles. The fact that the words "at Ephesus" (verse 1) in some early manuscripts are omitted is of little significance in view of the general character of the letter itself. Possibly this Epistle may be the letter to the Laodiceans (Col. 4:16)—that is, the letter may have been written as a circular, or encyclical, going to various churches which each, in turn, was charged to pass on to another, with Ephesus as a final destination.

Though now but an insignificant village, in Paul's day Ephesus was the capital of Proconsular Asia, located on the Sacred Port and the river Cayster, and noted for its theater and its temple — the temple of Artemis (Diana)—both of which are mentioned in the Scriptures (Acts 19:27-29).

In addition to the text of the letter itself, much New Testament Scripture bears directly, or indirectly, on this city and the believers therein. It will be remembered that in his first missionary journey about A.D. 51, the Apostle was "forbidden to preach the word in Asia" (Acts 16:6), but returning from that journey, accompanied by Priscilla and Aquila of Rome, he stopped at Ephesus (Acts 18:18-21); and, upon resuming his journey, he left Priscilla and Aquila in Ephesus. This, Paul's first visit to Ephesus, was exceedingly brief yet vitally effective and apparently without opposition from the Jews in whose synagogue he "reasoned." Acts 20:31 records Paul's second visit, about A.D. 54, and indicates an unbroken ministry of three years (Acts 20:31); first for a period of three months in the synagogue, and later for a period of two years in the "school of one Tyrannus" (Acts 19:8-10). The beginning of this second ministry in Ephesus was characterized by his discovery of twelve men, disciples of John the Baptist, whom he led into the knowledge of Christ and who were rebaptized "into the name of the Lord Jesus." So far-reaching were the effects of the second visit that "all which dwelt in Asia heard the word of the Lord Jesus, both Jews and Greeks." This ministry accompanied by miracles so penetrated the thought of the heathen city that we are told "many of them also which used curious arts brought their books together, and burned them before all men, and they counted the price of them, and found it fifty thousand pieces of silver. So mightily grew the word of God and prevailed" (Acts 19:19, 20).

A Companion Text

Outside this Epistle to the Ephesians, perhaps the most important scripture bearing on the ministry of Paul in Ephesus will be found in Acts 20:17-38, which context records the farewell words of Paul to the elders of the Church at Ephesus. The Apostle, being restricted in time, stopping but briefly at Miletus on his way to Jerusalem, called for the elders to journey the thirty miles that he might be with them all the available time. This portion of Scripture (Acts 20:17-21, 25-38) should be read with care and compared with the message of the Ephesian letter. It is as follows:

"And from Miletus he sent to Ephesus, and called the elders of the church. And when they were come to him, he said unto them, Ye know, from the first day that I came into Asia, after what manner I have been with you at all seasons, serving the Lord with all humility of mind, and with many tears, and temptations, which befell me by the lying in wait of the Jews: and how I kept back nothing that was profitable unto you, but have shewed you, and have taught you publicly, and from house to house, testifying both to the Jews, and also to the Greeks, repentance toward God, and faith toward our Lord Jesus Christ . . . And now, behold, I know that ye all, among whom I have gone preaching the kingdom of God, shall see my face no more. Wherefore I take you to record this day, that I am pure from the blood of all men. For I have not shunned to declare unto you all the counsel of God. Take heed therefore unto yourselves, and to all the flock, over the which the Holy Ghost hath made you overseers, to feed the church of God, which he hath purchased with his own blood. For I know this, that after my departing shall grievous wolves enter in among you, not sparing the flock. Also of your own selves shall men arise, speaking perverse things, to draw away disciples after them. Therefore watch, and remember, that by the space of three years I ceased not to warn every one night and day with tears. And now, brethren, I commend you to God, and to the word of his grace, which is able to build you up, and to give you an inheritance among all them which are sanctified. I have coveted no man's silver, or gold, or apparel. Yea, ye yourselves know, that these hands have ministered unto my necessities, and to them that were with me. I have shewed you all things, how that so laboring ye ought to support the weak, and to remember the words of the Lord Jesus, how he said, It is more blessed to give than to receive. And when he had thus spoken, he kneeled down, and prayed with them all. And they all wept sore, and fell on Paul's neck, and kissed him, sorrowing most of all for the words which he spake, that they should see his face no more. And they accompanied him unto the ship."

From Ephesus Paul's first letter to the Corinthians was written, and the influence of the scenes which surrounded him is discernible (1 Cor. 4:9; 9:24, 25; 15:32). Later on, in A.D. 63, the Apostle's care for the Ephesian church is seen again in the various references to Ephesus in the Pastoral Epistles (1 Tim. 1:3; 2 Tim. 1:18; 4:12).

Events in Ephesus

We are also assured that, following the death of the Apostle Paul, both Peter and John carried on the apostolic testimony in the region of Ephesus. There John's Gospel and his Epistles were written. So, also, the Revelation was written from Patmos—removed from Ephesus but sixty miles. At Ephesus, likewise, the great Christian council which dealt with the Nestorian heresy was held in A.D. 431. But, finally, the Ephesian church is distinguished as the first of the seven churches to which the ascended and glorified Christ spoke through John. No accusation is made against her other than that she had lost her first love; on the other hand, she is commended by these priceless words: "I know thy works, and thy labor, and thy patience, and how thou canst not bear them which are evil: and thou hast tried them which say they are apostles, and are not, and hast found them liars: and hast borne, and hast patience, and for my name's sake hast labored, and hast not fainted. But this thou hast, that thou hatest the deeds of the Nicolaitanes, which I also hate" (Rev. 2:2, 3, 6). Here some intimation is given of the wealth of the spiritual life and experience that obtained in the Ephesian church before her departure from her first love.

The church was jealous both for apostolic authority and for the brotherhood of the saints; which brotherhood has been so sadly divided and so despoiled by Nicolaitanism, *i.e.*, the division between laity and clergy and the subverting of the laity by the clergy. The Epistle to the Ephesians reflects nothing of Nicolaitanism, though the ministry gifts are recorded (Eph. 4:11). It is in this Epistle that we read, "There is one body, and one Spirit, even as ye are called in one hope of your calling; one Lord, one faith, one baptism, one God and Father of all, who is above all, and through all, and in you all" (Eph. 4: 4-6). Similarly, as an introduction to the Epistle to the Ephesians this, the first letter to the churches in Asia, should be read with care, remembering that it is written by the Apostle John a full thirty years after the death of the Apostle Paul.

To Whom Addressed?

That the Epistle to the Ephesians is not addressed to unregenerate persons is clear. The full identification of the distinct and limited class to whom this message is addressed will be disclosed as the study of the Epistle proceeds. However, a brief identification of this particular company is called for at this point before the Epistle itself is approached. That this company may be seen in all its relationships and separate characteristics, a brief panorama of human history, past, present, and future, is here given.

Generally speaking, the period from Adam to Abraham, though occupying but the first eleven chapters of the Bible and including at least two thousand years, represents one-third of all human history as that history has progressed from Adam to the present time. The second period of two thousand years, or from Abraham to Christ, occupies by far the major portion of the text of the Bible; while the third period of nearly two thousand years, or from Christ to the present time, occupies a portion, but not all, of the New Testament. Prophecy plainly anticipates a yet future period of one thousand years, after which there will be the setting up of the new heavens and the new earth wherein dwelleth righteousness.

It is obvious that in the first period of two thousand years, though there were distinct nations, the earth was inhabited by one stock or kind of humanity; and in the second period of two thousand years, there were two distinct kinds of people—the original Gentile looking backward to federal headship in Adam, and the Jew looking backward to federal headship in Abraham (Heb. 7:9, 10). The seed of Abraham was to be different in kind, preservation, and destiny.

Three Classes of People

In this third period of two thousand years there are certainly three classes of people in the earth. The original Adamic stock and the Abrahamic stock are still here; but, added to these, or rather taken from them, not by natural generation, but by regeneration, there is a third group of people who look backward only to the resurrection of the last Adam, Christ, and these *in Him* and together *with Him* form the New Creation. Representatives of this third group have been present in the world in each generation during the period from Pentecost to the present hour. Representatives will also be present in each future generation until their elect number is completed, when they will be received into glory at the coming of Christ to receive His bride. The Apostle Paul clearly recognized the three classes of people of this period when he wrote: "Give none offense, neither to the Jews, nor to the Gentiles, nor to the church of God" (1 Cor. 10:32). Likewise, in Ephesians 2:11 the Apostle refers to the Gentiles as the *"Uncircumcision,"* and the Jews as the *"Circumcision in the flesh made by hands."* But in Colossians 2:11 he refers to the Church as *"the Circumcision made without hands."*

The same Apostle gives a most vivid statement of the Gentile's position in the world: "Wherefore remember, that ye being in time past Gentiles in the flesh, who are called Uncircumcision by that which is called the Circumcision in the flesh made by hands; that at that time ye were without Christ, being aliens from the commonwealth of Israel, and strangers from the covenants of promise, having no hope, and without God in the world" (Eph. 2:11, 12). He gives also the position of the Jew in the world: "Who are Israelites; to whom pertaineth the adoption, and the glory, and the covenants, and the giving of the law, and the service of God, and the promises; whose are the fathers, and of whom as concerning the flesh Christ came, who is over all, God blessed for ever. Amen" (Rom. 9:4, 5). In like manner, he states the position of the Church: "Blessed be the God and Father of our Lord Jesus Christ, who hath blessed us with every spiritual blessing in heavenly places in Christ: according as he hath chosen us in him before the foundation of the world, that we should be holy and without blame before him in love: having predestinated us unto the adoption of children by Jesus Christ unto himself, according to the good pleasure of his will, to the praise of the glory of his grace, wherein he hath made us accepted in the beloved" (Eph. 1:3-6).

Every student of the Scriptures will do well to ponder these passages carefully, both for the truth each portion contains as well as for the wide variation in privilege and position which each sets forth.

The Meaning of "Church"

Since it so vitally determines the right understanding of the Ephesian Epistle, the precise Biblical meaning of the word *Church* should be given careful consideration.

In the original word *Church* means a *called out assembly of people,* a meaning not unlike the English word *congregation,* or *gathering of people in one place.* Such was Israel in the wilderness (Acts

7:38), and such was the mob in the Ephesian theater, which mob is termed an *ekklesia,* or *church* (Acts 19:32). Of such companies it could never be said that the life of each individual of the company is hid with Christ in God, or that, collectively, they form the very Body of Christ; nor can these holy distinctions be applied to any organized church or congregation. The true Church is composed of all the redeemed who have been, or will be saved through Christ in the period between the day of Pentecost and the removal of the Church, which is yet to be (1 Thess. 4:13-18). That the true Church is not restricted to Jews, Gentiles, a sect, or to one generation is obvious. Each person in this heavenly company is individually called of God, regenerated, forgiven all trespasses, justified, made a member of the household and family of God, united to Christ, and destined to partake of His heavenly glory forever.

That the distinctive character of the Church may be still more clearly observed, the panoramic view of the divinely revealed program for the human family in the earth should be traced to its consummation. It will be seen from the Scriptures that, following the close of this age and the removal of the Church from the earth, there are to be but two classes of people—the Jew and the Gentile—in the earth during the coming period of a thousand years. Likewise, following this thousand-year period, and during the eternity of the new earth, the Jew, of necessity, will be on the earth; for their five great earthly covenants, which are everlasting, cannot be broken. These covenants concern their national entity (Isa. 66:22; Jer. 31:36), the lion of their land (Gen. 13:15), their throne (2 Sam. 7:16), their King (Jer. 33:21), and their Kingdom (Dan. 7:14); and, in like manner, Revelation 21:23-27 seems to indicate the continuation of redeemed nations on the earth in that eternity to come.

Truth for All

The Ephesian letter, though it is addressed to the one local church in Ephesus, contains truth which belongs to the whole company of those who are saved in this dispensation. This fact is disclosed in the two opening verses.

The Epistle opens with this clear identification of its author, "Paul, an apostle of Jesus Christ by the will of God." The name

Paul, or Paulus, is a Gentile name, while its Hebrew form is Saul, or Saulus. That he is an Apostle is one of the highest of honors, which honor is claimed here by the Apostle Paul, not at all in self-seeking, but as the ground of authority upon which he is about to write. He is God's messenger according to God's will, and those who, with humbleness of mind, will listen for God's voice, will give heed to the words of an Apostle (1 Cor. 9:1, 2; 2 Cor. 12:12; Gal. 1:1).

The Epistle is written to "the saints which are at Ephesus and to the faithful [full of faith, trustful] in Christ Jesus." Since the words *saint* and *sanctify* are from the same root, it follows that all who are saints are sanctified (Heb. 10:10, 14); that is, they have been set apart unto God—which is the true meaning of *sanctification*—by virtue of their union with Christ through the baptism with the Spirit. It follows, also, that those who are positionally sanctified, or set apart unto God through their union with Christ, which is true of every believer, are saints. After this manner, the message is addressed not only to saints who are in Ephesus, but to all the faithful in Christ Jesus. Thus the letter becomes a personal word to every child of God.

Section Two

Ephesians 1:3

3 Blessed be the God and Father of our Lord Jesus Christ, who hath blessed us with all spiritual blessings in heavenly places in Christ.

In the salutation of the Ephesian letter the Apostle Paul is identified as its human author, and those to whom he writes are addressed as, first the saints whose earthly abode is Ephesus, but whose spiritual position is *in Christ Jesus*. Secondly, the message is tended to all the faithful everywhere and anywhere who are *in Christ Jesus*.

Being thus addressed only to those who are saved, three distinct lines of truth inhere in the Epistle: (1) the present exalted position of each born-again believer; (2) the specific truth relative to the Church which is Christ's Body; and (3) the consistent walk and warfare of those who are saved.

Again, the *order* of truth as presented in this Epistle should be observed with care. True to the plan of divine grace, the Epistle first presents the believer's exalted position which has been secured through the infinite mercy and power of God, and this is followed by an appeal to the one thus favored to walk worthy of the calling wherewith he is called. Thus, in the divine plan, the walk, or manner of daily life, is seen to be a normal result, or reasonable expression, growing out of the possession of the exceeding riches of grace in Christ Jesus.

It cannot be too strongly emphasized that, under God's provision in grace, God must first accomplish by His own unaided power *all* that enters into the believer's postion in Christ and secure it forever; then, after this is accomplished, the saved one is called upon to live as one should live who has already entered the most exalted abiding position to which any created being could ever be brought. Naturally, the human heart with its ideals of personal merit and appreciation of common justice has always had a different conception. Is it not the usual plan to ask children to be good and then to reward them according to their effort?

Life Under the Law

Was not this God's way of dealing with Israel under the law when they were before Him as mere minors and under tutors and governors? And shall we dare to believe that a new plan has been secured through the death and resurrection of Christ and the present ministry of the Spirit wherein God perfectly and eternally saves the trusting sinner apart from every consideration of his merit or demerit, and that He does all this before any appeal for the daily life is made? Are we to believe also that this appeal, when it is made, is based only on the fact of a perfect merit already secured *in Christ?* Is it true that to be good because we *are saved* is even a stronger motive than to be good because we *hope* thereby to be saved? Satan has ever sought to confuse the weak believer at this crucial point by laying upon his conscience the responsibility of his *walk* before that believer has a true conception of his *standing* in Christ—from which standing everything that is vital in his walk must proceed.

In Christ

Certainly the first step for each child of God is to see himself as standing perfectly in the righteousness of God, that imputed righteousness which is gained by his position *in Christ* and to which nothing could ever be added in time or eternity. When the conscience is thus set free from the unbearable burden of human responsibility, namely, the providing of perfect merit in the sight of God, and is purged from dead works through the blood of Christ (Heb. 9:14), there is opened up to the mind and heart of the one thus enlightened the new sphere of liberty which belongs to the sons of God—liberty, indeed, to do according to the desire of the heart; but invariably these desires are to be accompanied by a right adjustment to the mind and will of God, for God is always working in a yielded heart "both to will and to do of his good pleasure" (Phil. 2:13).

In beginning the verse-by-verse contemplation of this Epistle, we shall find that the first section (Chapters 1, 2, and 3) contains no word of exhortation as to the believer's daily life, nor is any mention made of the service which he should render to God. The section is characterized by the revelation of the boundless work of God in behalf of one who trusts in Christ. Since the salutation occupies the first two verses of the letter, the message of the Epistle begins properly with verse 3:

"Blessed be the God and Father of our Lord Jesus Christ."

God is not only the *source* of every blessing, but He is the *object* of all our thanksgiving, worship and praise. The word here translated *blessed* is found eight times in the New Testament and is addressed only to God. It is an ascription of supreme worship in which all devotion and adoration that the human heart can give is ascribed to the God and Father of our Lord Jesus Christ. He is revealed to us by and through His Son; but according to the following Scriptures, the contemplation should not stop with the Son alone; it should lead on to the Father:

"All things are delivered unto me of my Father: and no man knoweth the Son, but the Father: neither knoweth any man the Father, save the Son, and he to whomsoever the Son will reveal him" (Matt. 11:27); "God . . . hath in these last days spoken unto us by his Son" (Heb. 1:1,2); "And whatsoever ye shall ask in my name, that will I do, that the Father may be glorified in the Son" (John 14:13). Never should we fail to glory in the Son; but it is an indication of spiritual immaturity if the Son has not led us on to the knowledge of the Father. The Son would have us join in adoration to the Father, for the Father is blessed indeed.

This Epistle could hardly begin upon a more exalted plane, nor could it assume more maturity of spiritual enlightenment in the ones to whom it is addressed. Recognizing the wisdom of the Apostle Paul in adapting his message to the capability of those to whom he writes we may conclude that the Ephesian saints were enriched in all things and, to an exceptional degree, were able to receive the "strong meat" of the Word. In undertaking an exposition of these themes, there should be no lessening of their high character even though simplicity in style is so much to be desired.

The phrase, "The God and Father of our Lord Jesus Christ," is the full title of the First Person of the Blessed Trinity, and it incorporates, also, the full title of the Second Person. True, God the Father is also the Father of all who believe, but for all eternity to come He must first be recognized by that surpassing distinction which, in part, has been His throughout the eternity past, namely, "The *God* and *Father* of our Lord Jesus Christ." The relation of the Second Person to the First Person has from all eternity been that of a Son, and, like all else related to the Godhead, it is not only eternal but unchangeable. He did not become a Son of the Father by His incarnation, nor by His resurrection, nor is He a Son by mere title, nor is He temporarily assuming such a relationship that He may execute His part in the Covenant of Redemption. He was the *Only Begotten* of the Father from all eternity, having no other relation to time and creation than that He is the Creator of them. It is evident that the Father and Son relationship sets forth only the features of *emanation* and *manifestation* and does not include the usual conception of derivation, inferiority, or distinction as to the time of beginning. The Son, being very God, is eternally on an absolute equality with the Father.

The Incarnation

On the other hand, the First Person became the God of the Second Person by the incarnation. Only from His humanity could Christ address the First Person as "My God." This He did in that moment of supreme manifestation of His humanity when on the cross He said, "My God, my God, why hast thou forsaken me?" And again, after His resurrection He said, "I ascend unto my Father and your Father; and to my God, and your God" (John 20:17).

When contemplating the full title of the First Person of the Godhead, 2 Corinthians 1:3 and 1 Peter 1:3 should be observed sufficiently to note the significance of the use of this phrase in each instance (note, also, Matt 27:46; 1 Cor. 3:23; Eph. 1:17; and Rev. 3:12).

Spiritual Blessings

"Who hath blessed us with all spiritual blessings in the heavenly *places* in Christ Jesus." As it is becoming for us to love Him "because he first loved us" (1 John 4:19), it is equally becoming that we should bless Him because He has first blessed us, and the infinity of His love does not surpass the infinity of His blessing; for the blessing includes "every spiritual blessing in the heavenly in Christ Jesus." Thus three qualifying conditions are set up with regard to the exalted character of those blessings the believer has now received, each of which reaches on into knowledge-surpassing realms.

(1) The spiritual blessings are not limited to the unseen as in distinction to the seen, nor to the immaterial as in distinction to the material; the thought expressed being that these blessings come forth from God and not from humanly devised circumstances. There is a reiteration here of the great fact so clearly stated by Jonah when he said, "Salvation is of the Lord" (Jonah 2:9); and again stated by the Apostle Paul, "By the grace of God I am what I am" (1 Cor. 15:10). From all this it will be seen that, though man possesses a strange power by which he may hinder the work of God, he, on the other hand, is as strangely impotent in the realms of spiritual attainment.

(2) These divine blessings are identified as belonging to the *heavenly*. The term *heavenly* is an adjective without a noun, and the human mind naturally seeks to discover what it is that is here said to be *heavenly*. *Heavenly* is a term which is peculiar to the Ephesian letter (as the phrase *the kingdom of heaven* is peculiar to Matthew's Gospel); it occurs also in 2:6, 3:10, and 6:12. The translators of our Authorized Version have supplied the noun *places*. This would imply that some localities are more blessed than others. Some interpreters have suggested that these blessings are heavenly because of the fact that they originate in, and proceed from heaven.

Still another interpretation, which has very much in its favor, is that reference is here made to the *sphere* of the believer's present relation to Christ. This sphere of relationship is far-reaching and all-inclusive. It includes the sharing of the divine nature; the possession of life which is none other than "Christ begotten in you the hope of glory"; the common purpose with Christ in service indicated by the words, "As thou hast sent me into the world, even so have I also sent them into the world"; the relation between Christ and the believer as forming the New Creation; in suffering, for we suffer together with Him; in inheritance, for it is said that we are "joint-heirs with Christ"; and in a yet future glory, when we shall be "glorified together with Him." Such a sphere of blessing is not limited to favored places but is ever and always the deepest reality in the unchanging sphere of identity with Christ, a reality which can shed its radiant glories in the human heart even in the dungeon at midnight as much as in the blazing glory of celestial realms.

(3) In His upper-room discourse, Christ uttered a phrase of seven monosyllables which sets forth the major twofold characterization of the Christian—"Ye in me, and I in you" (John 14:20). Judging from these seven words alone, how marvelous are the inexhaustible and unsearchable riches of divine grace, and yet how wonderful is the simplicity of the divine utterance! The second of these two relationships, stated in the words, "I in you," asserts the essential truth that the child of God has received a new impartation of life, which life is none other than the indwelling Christ. The fact of a new *impartation* of Christ's life should not be contemplated as being a mere *imitation* of Christ, or a new *rule* or *ideal* of life, it is "Christ in you, the hope of glory." The Christian is one to whom Christ has given His own eternal life, which truth is sustained by no less than eighty New Testament passages, and to which Christ referred when He said, "I give unto them eternal life" (John 10:23), and, in like manner, when He said, "I in you."

"Ye in me"

The first of these two phrases—"ye in me"—is the one which is referred to in Ephesians 1:3, and which, more than all else, discloses the basis on which the knowledge surpassing heavenly blessings rest, as well as the ground on which they are bestowed.

The whole theme of the New Creation is compressed in these three words of two letters each. As the entire unregenerate race is in *Adam* and constituted sinners by his one act of disobedience (Rom. 5:19), so the entire regenerate group are *in Christ* and are constituted righteous by His one act of obedience. Likewise, because of its relation to Adam, the first creation became subject to death; so, also, the New Creation, because of its relation to Christ, has received the gift of God which is eternal life; and, added to this, all heavenly blessings which are in Christ Jesus. The limitless scope of these heavenly blessings has been pointed out above. It remains to be seen that the release of this transforming divine favor is granted, not on the ground of any fancied or real personal qualities attained or attainable, but is bestowed on the ground of the fact that God now sees the believer as transferred from the ruin of the Old Creation into the riches of the New Creation. By the gracious baptizing work of the Holy Spirit the believer, at the moment he is saved, is joined to Christ and is then eternally delivered from every complication and condemnation arising out of the first Adamic headship. Similarly, and at the same time, he is made to partake of every spiritual blessing in the heavenly association in Christ Jesus. Therefore, it may be said of the least of the children of God that he not only possesses the indwelling Christ, Who is his eternal life, but he is ensphered *in Christ* and thus enriched with all that Christ is and all that Christ has received. These riches are beyond comprehension; they include not only that infinite grace and perfection which Christ offered to God in our behalf, but they include also, all that He received from the Father (John 16:15), and all that was conferred upon Him because of the fact that He was obedient unto death—an incomparable glory (Phil. 2:9). The human mind cannot comprehend such riches. Nevertheless, according to the testimony of the Scriptures, the child of God is now a partaker of all these riches *in Christ Jesus*. Added to this, these divine benefits are made real to the believer's heart and mind by the illuminating work of the Spirit (John 16:11-15).

Certain major aspects of these riches are emphasized in the Scriptures: the believer is "made the righteousness of God in him" (2 Cor. 5:21); he is "accepted in the beloved" (Eph. 1:6); he is "in Christ Jesus . . . made nigh" (Eph. 2:13); he is loved as Christ is loved (John 17:23); he is no longer of this world (John 17:16); and he is heard when he prays, as though his voice were the voice of the Son of God (John 14:14).

It remains yet to observe that all these marvels (and the half has never been told) are the *immediate* and *present possession* of every one that is saved. This fact is set forth with great emphasis. Our God and Father *hath* blessed us with every spiritual blessing in the heavenly association in Christ Jesus, and to those who trust in Christ, though they deserve in themselves only eternal condemnation, it is said, "all things are yours" (1 Cor. 3:21), and, "ye are complete in him" (Col. 2:10).

Section Three

Ephesians 1:4-6

4   According as he hath chosen us in him before the foundation of the world, that we should be holy and without blame before him in love:
5   Having predestinated us unto the adoption of children by Jesus Christ to himself, according to the good pleasure of his will,
6   To the praise of the glory of his grace, wherein he hath made us accepted in the beloved.

The previous study in this series was largely occupied with one verse (1:3) wherein is recorded the word of praise to the Father for His measureless spiritual blessings in Christ Jesus to all who believe. The section which follows and which is now to be considered (1:4-6) is the beginning of an enumeration and amplification of the heavenly positions which together constitute the present spiritual blessings mentioned in verse 3.

Attention has been called to the spiritual insight which characterized the Ephesian believers, and at no point in this Epistle is the fact of their understanding of the deep things of God more demonstrated than that this portion now to be considered was addressed to them. So deeply theological is this section of the Epistle that no little strain is placed upon the expositor whose ideal is a degree of simplicity of expression suited to the understanding of the average Christian. The enumeration of these heavenly positions presents a series of fundamental doctrines—doctrines which have engaged the greatest minds in all ages—and, though presenting certain facts regarding the believer's position *in Christ*, this Scripture does not set forth an

31

exhaustive list of *all* these positions, nor will a complete list be found at any one place in the New Testament.

Only the briefest consideration can be given here to the positions that are mentioned in this section of the Epistle.

"Chosen in Him Before the Foundation of the World."

What could be more orderly than that the contemplation of the divine dealing with man should begin with a declaration of God's sovereignty in election? Whatever God bestows upon His creatures must, of necessity, be absolute in its nature. He here discovers nothing in fallen man other than an *object* of His super-abounding grace. The first man, Adam, stood before God on the ground of a *natural perfection*, being the true representation of God's creative purpose; but Adam fell from the estate of natural perfection and from that time, both for Adam and his posterity, only *regenerative* grace could commend any human being to God. No obligation rests upon God in the exercise of His grace. He may, and does, choose whom He will. He neither sees, nor foresees, any good in man which might form a basis of His blessings.

Whatever good is found in redeemed man is wrought in him by divine grace. God does design for those whom He chooses that they shall be "holy and without blame before him"; but this is the result which is wrought by God in grace, and is never wrought by man. Certainly man has not chosen God. Christ emphasized this when He said, "Ye have not chosen me, but I have chosen you." Even the first man when unfallen and wholly free to choose did not choose God; how much more is it certain that fallen man will not of himself choose God! Therefore the provision of the ground of redemption is not enough in itself; the perverted will of man must be divinely moved. The unregenerate heart must be rendered willing as well as transformed in its essential character. All this God undertakes and accomplishes in sovereign grace. He elects, He calls, He inclines the heart, He redeems, He regenerates, He preserves, and He presents faultless before His glory those who are the objects of His sovereign grace.

On the other hand, He employs means to the accomplishment of His purpose. On the divine side, the awful demands of sin must be met by the sacrifice of His only begotten Son. It is not enough that sin shall be *declared* to be sinful; it is required that its curse shall be *borne* by the Lamb of God, the will of man must be moved, regeneration must be wrought by the Spirit, and every spiritual and heavenly blessing must be secured by the setting up of an actual union with Christ. On the human side, when man's opposition to God is divinely broken down, he then believes to the saving of his soul. So demanding and real are all the divine means employed for the saving of the lost, that it is as much required of man that he believe and thus elect to be saved by the divine grace as that actual redemption shall be wrought for him on Calvary's cross. In the realm of human experience man is conscious only of his power to choose, or reject, the salvation that is in Christ; and, because of the reality of this human choice, he is saved or lost according to his belief, or disbelief, in Christ as his Savior.

While there is very much in the doctrine of divine election which transcends the limitations of the finite understanding, it is true that man originates nothing—not even sin, since sin began with the angels of God. It is God who has chosen His elect, and while this selection is both sovereign and final, nevertheless, not one human being who desires to be saved and who complies with the necessary terms of the gospel will ever be lost.

Though the doctrine of divine election presents difficulties which are insolvable by the finite mind, the fact of divine selection is not limited to God's choice of some out of the many for eternal glory; it is observable anywhere in the universe. There is a variety in all God's creation. There are classifications among the angels. One star is said to differ from another star in glory. Men are not born of the same race with the same advantages, nor with the same native abilities. These variations in the estates of men cannot be accounted for on the basis of the efficacy of the free will of man. Men do not choose their race, their life conditions (whether it be in civilization or in heathendom), nor do they choose their natural gifts. On the other hand, it is as clearly disclosed to those who will receive the revelation, that God's attitude toward the entire human family is one of infinite compassion and boundless sacrificial love.

Though the two revealed facts—divine election and the universality of divine love—cannot be reconciled within the sphere of human understanding, here, as elsewhere, we may honor God by *believing* and by *resting* in Him. Therefore, to God be all the glory!

And to Him be given the first consideration! Those systems of religious thought which required that the doctrine of God shall conform to the doctrine of the supremacy of man, which begin with man, defend man, and glorify man, are fundamentally wrong and therefore are productive of God-dishonoring error. The order of truth is established forever by the first phrase of the Bible, "In the beginning God." He it is Who planned, He executes, and He it is Who will realize to an infinite degree all that He has purposed. He will never be defeated nor disappointed. The true system of religious thought begins with God, defends God, and glorifies God; and the creature is conformed to the plan and purpose of the Creator. The fall of man alone can account for the wickedness of heart which resists the divine supremacy.

The divine selection of some for eternal glory was made before all time. The phrase, "before the foundation of the world," occurs also in John 17:24 and 1 Peter 1:20. In these passages the eternal feature is obvious. While there is a similar phrase, "from the foundation of the world" (Luke 11:50; Heb. 4:3; 9:26), meaning since the beginning of time, the phrase "before the foundation of the world" refers specifically to the eternity past (cf. 1 Cor. 2:7; 2 Tim. 1:9; Titus 1:2; Rom. 16:25). The eternal feature of God's elective choice is of measureless importance as a factor in the recognition of divine sovereignty. At a time and under conditions where there was none other than His Triune Self to determine and none other to satisfy or glorify, He determined the objects of His grace and decreed all the means necessary to the realization of His purpose. Deep indeed are the mysteries of the eternal counsels of God, yet it is to these mysteries that the Apostle refers at the opening of this letter, and upon these as a basis he proceeds with his exalted message addressed, as it is, to all the children of God.

"Having Predestinated Us."

Election and predestination do not indicate the same thing.

Election is God's selection of individuals, while predestination is His plan and purpose for those whom He selects. It is also to be observed that He predestinates nothing for those whom He does not elect for His eternal glory; but He does predestinate the destiny of those whom He chooses. The Apostle has already anticipated the fact of predestination in the preceding verse wherein the eternal purpose is said to be "that we should be holy and without blame before him." This utterance might refer to the state of those who are redeemed and who by divine grace are finally perfected into the image of Christ (1 John 3:3), or it might refer to the standing of the believer in Christ, in which union all the perfections of Christ are imputed to the believer for all eternity to come. The theme as introduced in verse 3 would favor the latter interpretation; for it is the heavenly, spiritual blessings in Christ which are in view. However, it is provided, and most engaging is the contemplation, that in his destiny and as a realization of divine election rather than by human attainment, the believer will be perfected in his state as he is now and forever perfected in his standing (cf. Rom. 8:29 with Heb. 10:14).

It is true that, in the execution of His purpose, God will both incline and draw those whom He chooses and provide for them the redemption by which alone they can be the objects of His blessing. But the earthly aspects of His purpose are not at this point in view; He is rather relating the past eternity with that eternity which is to come. Before the foundation of the world He made sovereign choice of those who in the eternity to come would be holy and without blame before Him. A similar passage occurs in Romans 8:30, "Moreover, whom he did predestinate, them he also called: and whom he called, them he also justified: and whom he justified, them he also glorified."

Here, again, the connection is set up between the predestination which characterized the eternity past, and the glory that will characterize the eternity to come. However, it is indicated here that to realize this end He both calls and justifies, and there is no failure or loss of one. All whom He predestinates He calls, all whom He calls He justifies, and all whom He justifies He glorifies. Let it be stated again, that this is truth on the highest conceivable plane where the sovereign election of God is alone presented with its certainty of fruition. Its realization called for the creation of worlds, the creation of man, the permission of evil, the fall, the ages of human history, redemption at infinite cost, and the calling and justifying of His elect; but the end is sure. It will be in the end precisely what He decreed it to be in the beginning. Later in this Epistle it will be seen (Eph. 2:7) that this purpose is not for the display of His holy judgments in the retribution of those who do not believe, though that retribution is unavoidable, but it is for the manifestation of His grace in those who do believe. Thus His love is the dominating motive in all that He does. For this reason it is probably correct to relate the phrase "in love" which occurs at the end of verse 4 with the beginning of verse 5. It is in love that He predestinated us.

Love is one of the attributes of God. "God is love," which means that He has never acquired love, He does not maintain it by any effort whatsoever, nor does His love depend upon conditions; for He is the Author of all conditions. God loved before any being was created, and at a time—if time it be—when there was no other than His own Triune Being. He loved Himself supremely, but upon a plane far above that of mere self-complacency. His love is as eternal and unchangeable as His own existence, and it was in that incomprehensible past that He also loved the beings He would yet create. Though expressed supremely by the death of Christ at a moment in time, and though seen in the preservation of, and providence over, His redeemed, His is a love of the dateless past and its continuation is as immutable as the predestination it devises. Yes, predestination is, so far from being a hard and awful predetermination of God, in reality, the supreme undertaking and satisfaction of His infinite compassion.

Only one aspect of His predetermining purpose is mentioned in this passage: it is, "unto the adoption of children by Jesus Christ to himself according to the good pleasure of his will," and thus *adoption* is exalted to a place among the heavenly, spiritual blessings in Christ. Two features of filial relation to God the Father through Christ should be distinguished: there is, first, that aspect of *relationship* which results from regeneration and involves the change of estate and nature and provides a right and title to all riches of divine favor; and there is, second, that aspect of *position* which has to do with privilege.

In human life, relationship with all its realities is accorded the child from his birth to the day he reaches his majority. After that, though relationship is unchanged, he enters a sphere of freedom, responsibility and prerogative. So, in like manner, the believer is constituted a legitimate child of God by spiritual birth with all its attending relationships, but he is also, at the moment of that birth, advanced to maturity of position, being constituted an adult son by virtue of that legal placing which in the Scriptures is termed adoption. Being free from the law, the child of God is no longer "under tutors and governors" as was Israel (Gal. 4:1-3), but is rather called to the liberty and freedom which is in Christ Jesus (Gal. 5:1). There is therefore no childhood period in the sphere of the Christian's responsibility. Whatever appeal as to a holy walk and service God addresses to one He addresses to all regardless of the length of time they may have been saved.

"Made accepted in the Beloved."

"The Beloved" is none other than Christ, Who is so named because He is beloved of His Father, and, while He is beloved of the Father, He is, at the same time, despised and rejected by the world. The child of God will therefore contemplate his hope, not as related to this world, but as related to Christ in the heavenly realms. Thus, also, the Christian need anticipate no more from the world than is accorded Christ. "If they have hated me, they will hate you" and, "Ye are not of the world even as I am not of the world." But the present theme is not of that rejection which for a little time is promised here; it is rather of that acceptance forever which is even now the believer's position in heaven.

Precious indeed is the fact that the child of God is made accepted; the implication being, according to truth, that redeeming grace has so answered every judgment because of demerit, and so provided every essential quality through the merit of Another, that the Father sees the saved one in the standing of His Son and loves him as He loves His Son (John 17:23). All this is possible because divine grace and power have so wrought that the believer is made accepted in the Beloved.

Such a measureless accomplishment will not only serve the desirable purpose of a soul being perfectly saved for all eternity, but it will redound "to the praise of the glory of his grace." Again and again the Apostle returns to this final objective of salvation: it is that the glory of His grace may be praised. How high, then, is the calling which is ours. In the sovereign choice of God, we shall be employed as the instrumentality whereby He will disclose the eternal riches of His favor!

Section Four

Ephesians 1:7-14

7 In whom we have redemption through his blood, the forgiveness of sins, according to the riches of his grace;

8 Wherein he hath abounded toward us in all wisdom and prudence;

9 Having made known unto us the mystery of his will, according to his good pleasure which he hath purposed in himself:

10 That in the dispensation of the fulness of times he might gather together in one all things in Christ, both which are in heaven, and which are on earth; even in him:

11 In whom also we have obtained an inheritance, being predestinated according to the purpose of him who worketh all things after the counsel of his own will:

12 That we should be to the praise of his glory, who first trusted in Christ.

13 In whom ye also trusted, after that ye heard the word of truth, the gospel of your salvation: in whom also after that ye believed, ye were sealed with that Holy Spirit of promise,

14 Which is the earnest of our inheritance until the redemption of the purchased possession, unto the praise of his glory.

Resuming the connected theme presented in the opening verses of the Ephesian letter, we enter upon a section (1:7-14) wherein the writer descends from the premundane purposes of God, unfolded in the preceding portion, to the actual execution of those upon the earth and within the boundaries of time. Here again, not every aspect of the divine activity is enumerated, but only such of these as will serve to indicate the precise nature of the divine undertaking.

As has been stated in the previous study, the divine purpose anticipates a well-defined, predetermined end for those whom, as sons, He will bring into glory. The process by which the predetermined end will be reached is manifold in its particulars, incorporating, as it does, every minute detail of divine action and human experience intervening between the originating, sovereign choice of an elect company, in the past eternity, and the final presentation of that company in glory in the eternity to come.

The execution of this vast program necessitated the creation of all things. In Colossians 1:16, it is declared that "all things were created by him, and for him," which creation includes the heavenly hosts, and things "that are in heaven, and that are in earth, visible and invisible, whether they be thrones, or dominions, or principalities, or powers." Likewise, in Ephesians 1:23 and 5:27, it is revealed that this elect company is the supreme object of the affections of the One for Whom and by Whom all things were created and for whom He has made the supreme sacrifice.

An Object of Divine Grace

According to the divine plan, man is the highest in position and capacity of all earthly creation and in his original estate reflected perfectly and properly the holy character and sublime creative power of God; but, as originally created, man did not serve as a manifestation of the grace of God. Being unfallen and fulfilling to satisfaction the ideal of his Maker, man was not, nor could he then be, an object of divine grace. In this connection it should be observed that the precise scope of divine grace as revealed in the Word of God is not that general benevolence toward man which doubtless characterized the attitude of God toward unfallen man: it is rather that exercise of mercy toward the sinner who is otherwise doomed, which mercy has been made possible through Christ's death as the sinner's Substitute bearing his justly imposed condemnation. Likewise, it should be observed that, when man fell, he descended to a level so low that he became only and forever an object of divine grace.

So long as virtue and goodness have existed, their opposite, evil, has been at least a conceivable thing, though without the slightest possibility of expression before the creation of angels and man. But the problem as to why sin was ever permitted its manifestation either in heaven by Satan or on earth by man is an insoluble mystery to the finite mind and is no more disclosed in this portion of Scripture than elsewhere. There can be no question but what the expression of sin was divinely permitted. It did not come as a surprise to God, nor did it frustrate His purpose. It must be remembered, also, that sin was permitted in spite of the fact that it is so abhorrent to God and in spite of the fact that its tragedy could be healed only by the most costly sacrifice possible to God —the death of His Son.

While He permitted sin in the universe, God is not disclosed as being responsible for it. He is rather revealed as the One Who hates it with a perfect hatred. However, the problem is not without a partial solution. There was that in God which had never been expressed, nor could it be expressed until sin had entered the world. His wisdom, His power, and His glory had been disclosed by created things (Ps. 19:1; Rom. 1:19, 20); but until there were fallen beings, no manifestation of the compassion of God was possible. How gracious He could be to a hell-deserving sinner could not be demonstrated until such an object of His grace existed. A soul tested in the furnace of temptation and saved from eternal condemnation by divine grace will be a witness in heaven of that in God which otherwise could never have been made known. So great a salvation will redound "to the praise of the glory of his grace."

Thus the Apostle declares in verse 7 concerning Christ, "In whom we have redemption." Nothing is revealed of the preliminary fact that in and through the fall of the first Adam we have need of redemption. That need is assumed and is but a necessary step in the preparation of the more essential manifestation of super-abounding grace. In Christ Jesus we have redemption. On the divine side, the great redeeming work is accomplished. It is now a completed transaction; not a thing which God will do for man upon some condition of human worthiness, but a thing which He has done for man already and when man was without merit, without strength, a sinner, and an enemy of God. That there is an elect company in the divine view is no part of the gospel of divine grace which is addressed to a lost world; it is one of God's secrets intended only for those who are saved. On the other hand, the announcement of an accomplished blood-redemption as potentially provided for all is the evangel of infinite grace, "Whosoever will, may come."

Redemption has always been by blood alone. Blood is the divinely determined ransom which an outraged holiness must demand. That blood-ransom was prefigured in all Old Testament sacrifices as it is now available through the death of Christ; hence redemption has been offered to man as a benefit throughout the history of the race.

O Divine Redeemer

Having contemplated the holy nature of God and His uncompromising, unyielding character and government, it is not difficult to accept the solemn decree, "The soul that sinneth it shall die"; likewise, "The wages of sin is death"; and, again, "Without shedding of blood there is no remission." God never deals with sin in leniency or mere generosity. The awful penalty which sin inevitably incurs cannot be lessened in the slightest degree. God's holy demands which are based on His holy character are as unchangeable as His nature. Christ paid the required ransom. Divine justice is satisfied, and the way of salvation is now open for all. The responsibility imposed on the sinner is that of *believing* the record God has given concerning this redemption which is in His Son. This record points to the Redeemer as the only One who is *able* to save, and calls for nothing less or for nothing more than saving trust in Him. It is in Him that we have redemption. He *is* our redemption. By the shedding of His blood He accomplished a perfect ransom; by His resurrection He proved the completeness of His undertaking, and resumed His life by the same authority by which He laid it down. Thus He ever lives as the all-sufficient Redeemer of those for whom He died. It is God who in infinite grace provided a ransom, and it is man who in infinite sin rejects that ransom. The price *is* paid and the grace of God *is* the portion of each and every one who will receive it, and those who are saved can say with the Apostle, "We have redemption through his blood, the forgiveness of sins, according to the riches of his grace."

In the outworking of the plan of redemption, God has wrought on an infinite plane and has disclosed the unsearchable depths of His wisdom and prudence (1:8). In 1 Corinthians 1:23, 24, the great transaction of the sacrifice of Christ is declared to be the manifestation of divine power and wisdom. As revealed in the Scriptures, the greatest problem that ever confronted the Almighty is not creation, which in Psalm 8:3 is likened to mere finger-play: it is rather the redemption of a lost soul, which, according to Isaiah 53:1, required the making bare of His great right arm.

His *wisdom* is seen in the solving of the problem as to how God can remain just and yet be, according to the compassion of His heart, the *Justifier* of the sinner. His power is set free to act in behalf of all who believe on Christ as their Savior, and, when thus set free, He will not stop short of the satisfaction of His measureless love. He will present the saved one in glory conformed to the image of His Son.

God is satisfied with the payment Christ has made, and it is in Him who alone is worthy that we have a perfect redemption, even the forgiveness of sins: not, indeed, a partial forgiveness, which would be no manifestation of infinite grace, but that which, being complete forever, remains an abiding glory to God. Thus, the believer is accepted eternally into the family of the redeemed; yet, in that family relationship he will, time and again, need to be forgiven—in the sense of being restored, not into the family, but into the fellowship of the Father and the Son (1 John 1:9).

At this point in the progress of the Ephesian message (verse 9), one great example of the abounding grace and wisdom of God is stated, being addressed, as it is, to *all* who share in the redemption that is in Christ, and forming, as it does, a part of the New Testament revelation. The precise nature of the message is stated in the ensuing verse. However, the Apostle anticipates the nature of the message in two particulars: first, it is a *mystery*, and second, it is a *purpose* which the Father purposed in His Son (the phrase "in Himself" being better rendered, in Him, i.e., in Christ).

In the New Testament sense of the word, a *mystery* is a truth undiscoverable apart from revelation and usually refers to something not clearly disclosed in the Old Testament, but now revealed in the New Testament; even there it is not always completely set forth, enough being declared, however, to form a basis for identification and human compliance. To illustrate this: it is impossible for the human mind to grasp *all* that is involved in the resurrection of the dead and the translation of the living as stated in 1 Corinthians 15:51-52; but, though termed a mystery and not in these precise particulars seen in the Old Testament, enough is revealed to form the ground of a great hope and consolation. Such, in the main, is the character of all the New Testament mysteries. Together they form a most important division of truth and sum up largely the progress of revelation in the New Testament over that of the Old Testament.

A Mystery Revealed

According to verse 10, the mystery which the Father purposed in His Son is to be realized at a time which is here identified as "the dispensation of the fulness of times"; and since the word dispensation here means stewardship—the assuming and discharging with complete authority all the interests of another—the "dispensation of the fulness of times" is that yet future period when Christ will exercise headship authority over all things both in heaven and on earth. Since such headship is not being exercised in this age, nor has it been exercised in any past age, it is evident that another age for the realization of these divine purposes is determined which will follow the present period.

Not yet are all things put under the authority of the Son (Heb. 2:8; cf. 1 Cor. 15:25-28), nor could this authority be His until He returns, according to the promise, to govern the earth. The Father's commissioned One in the age of His stewardship will yet reign over all things. This will be the fulness, or consummation, of all preceding seasons. Human history, which throughout the ages has been characterized by incompleteness, is yet to see completeness in the stewardship of Christ. The Gentile nations will be enriched under the authority of the

Prince of Peace; Israel's great covenants will be fulfilled; and the Church will have been joined to the Lord and have experienced the fruition of all her promised heavenly blessings. The stewardship of the Son will gather under one authority all things that are in heaven and on earth. The revelation of this mystery transcends human understanding, but the hope and its certainty are assured.

The great disclosure that all authority is yet to be centered *in Christ* should not be confused with the present fact that the Church is now, as to spiritual, vital union, in Christ; the latter being the theme with which the Epistle opened. Enlarging upon this aspect of truth, in verse 11 the Apostle declares that *in Christ* the children of God *have obtained an inheritance*. They share by right in all that belongs to Christ. They are "heirs of God, and joint-heirs with Christ" (Rom. 8:17). All this, it is reiterated, is the fulfilling of the sovereign, divine predestination, and is according to the purpose of Him who worketh all things after the counsel of His own will. Thus, they (verse 12) who first trusted in Christ are to be to the praise of His glory. The trust, to which reference is here made, is not that saving faith by which they are constituted children of God; it is rather the reasonable expectation of the future association with Him in glory at His coming again.

After the refreshing return to the premundane purposes of God with the assurance that all things in heaven and on earth will be executed according to the counsel of His own will, the theme reverts again to earthly things and to the experience of the Ephesian believers in particular. They are reminded that they did trust in Christ after that they heard the Word of truth, the gospel of their salvation. To them, as to all God's elect, the gospel must be preached, and by them be received. How else will that be realized which is according to His purpose and after the counsel of *His will*?

The opening section of this Epistle (1:1-14), which carries the reader into both the eternity past and that which is to come, and which asserts the fact of sovereign, immutable, divine predestination, comes to its close with the mention of one more of the heavenly, spiritual blessings which accrue to the believer because of the fact that he is *in* Christ Jesus. As has been stated, the saved one is *chosen* in sovereign grace, *predestinated* in love, *adopted* into heaven-high privilege, *redeemed*, *illuminated*, made a *partaker* of Christ's *inheritance*, and, finally, *sealed* with that Holy Spirit of Promise.

Sealing of the Spirit

The sealing with the Holy Spirit of Promise is distinctly a sealing *in Christ*. This seal carries two important meanings:first, that of reality, and second, that of rightful ownership. As the sealing of the Spirit is again mentioned in 4:30, it will be observed that the present instance is unto reality (cf. John 3:33), and the later reference is unto rightful ownership. That there may be no possible doubt as to the reality of the believer's position *in Christ* he has been sealed therein by the Holy Spirit of Promise. This sealing took place not after, but upon believing. The Authorized text, "after that ye believed," is better rendered "upon believing." There is no reference here, or elsewhere in the Scriptures, to a second work of grace, nor is it once implied that these divine blessings are received in sequence; on the contrary, upon believing, the child of God is blessed with *every* spiritual blessing in the heavenly in Christ Jesus.

The Spirit is here distinguished as the Spirit of Promise since His advent into the world was covenanted by both the Father and the Son. He is holy to that degree which identifies Him with the Persons of the Trinity. He Himself is the earnest of our inheritance (verse 14) until the completion of our redemption. An earnest is a pre-payment, or foretaste of an oncoming bounty. Thus all the present blessed influences and ministries of the Spirit to the child of God are but an intimation of the boundless, experimental fulness of the inheritance which is yet to be. Divine illumination is needed if these marvels of grace are to be comprehended; hence, at this point, the Apostle turns to prayer.

Section Five

Ephesians 1:15-23

15 Wherefore I also, after I heard of your faith in the Lord Jesus, and love unto all the saints,

16 Cease not to give thanks for you, making mention of you in my prayers;

17 That the God of our Lord Jesus Christ, the Father of glory, may give unto you the spirit of wisdom and revelation in the knowledge of him:

18 The eyes of your understanding being enlightened; that ye may know what is the hope of his calling and what the riches of the glory of his inheritance in the saints,

19 And what is the exceeding greatness of his power to us-ward who believe, according to the working of his mighty power,

20 Which he wrought in Christ, when he raised him from the dead, and set him at his own right hand in the heavenly places,

21 Far above all principality, and power, and might, and dominion, and every name that is named, not only in this world, but also in that which is to come:

22 And hath put all things under his feet, and gave him to be the head over all things to the church,

23 Which is his body, the fulness of him that filleth all in all.

The author, the Apostle Paul, who from the salutation of this Epistle has been hidden from view by the magnitude of his theme, now, in verse 15, comes forward and the Epistle assumes again the character of a personal message. True to his gracious attitude, he finds abundant reason for joy in the contemplation of the Christian character already developed in those he had led to the saving knowledge of Christ. The report of their spiritual progress and steadfastness had been conveyed by one who had more recently observed the devoted lives of the Ephesian saints. Perhaps this message was received through Epaphras (Col. 1:7). Others, too, it is implied, joined with the Apostle in the joyful contemplation of this advancement in the knowledge of Christ. The advancement of the saints of Ephesus is both one of faith in the Lord Jesus, and love unto all the brethren, the latter being the logical result of the former.

The portion now under consideration (1:15-23) is closely related to that which has gone before; opening, as it does, with the connecting word, wherefore. In view of the divine purpose toward believers which has been set forth, the Apostle, at this point, testifies to them of his prayer on their behalf, which was to the end that they might be divinely enabled to comprehend these riches of grace and glory; but not until he has first given expression to his thanksgiving to God for the benefit they have received. Not once only is he exercised in prayer, but often. He declares that he "ceased not" to give thanks for them. Thus is provided one more evidence of the persevering character of the prayer ministry of the Apostle Paul. His faithfulness in prayer is most impressive, and his recorded prayers form some of the richest portions of the New Testament.

The Apostle prays that the God of our Lord Jesus Christ, the Father of Glory, may give unto them the spirit of wisdom and revelation in the knowledge of Himself. Thus, as in verse 3, he refers to the First Person of the Godhead as "the God of our Lord Jesus Christ," and here, as before, the humanity of Christ is in view; for only in that relationship is the First Person properly addressed as the God of the Second Person. In Matthew 27:46 it is recorded that in the hour of His death the Son so addressed the Father. It was necessary that the Son of God, in order that He might "taste death," should become incarnate, and there was no possible redemption apart from His death. In like manner, we have in John 20:17 a similar reference to the First Person on the part of the Second Person, but, in this case, after the resurrection. Naturally, there is great significance in this since it attests the fact that Christ retains His humanity in His present exaltation and forever.

The First Person is also addressed as "the Father of Glory."

The indisputable truth that He is a glorious Person is hardly the meaning here; it is rather the fact that glory is an attribute belonging to the very essence of God, which fact is far removed from the mere ascription to Him of glory on the part of others. There is a peculiar fitness in the use of the title "the Father of Glory" in a prayer the central thought of which is the display of the divine glory in and through Christ—who is the brightness of His excellent glory (Heb. 1:3); and it is further declared that the knowledge of the glory of God is seen in the face of Jesus Christ (2 Cor. 4:6). Thus, through the incarnation, that essential glory, like other aspects of deity, has been brought into the range of human contemplation.

To Know God

To know God in His perfections, as He is revealed in Christ (Col. 2:9), is the exalted privilege of believers; the human incapacity for such knowledge being overcome, in the divine provision, by the Spirit of God who is appointed to take of the things of Christ and *show* them unto us (John 16:12-15). Thus reference is made in verse 17 to the Spirit as "the Spirit of wisdom and revelation in the knowledge of him." The world is satisfied with the ideal expressed by the phrase, "know thyself"; but to the child of God it is given to know God, whom to know aright is life eternal. Significant, indeed, is the use of the Greek word *epigenosis* at this point, which word refers to a full knowledge, and is much stronger than the general word *genosis*, which refers to the more restricted aspects of human understanding. In Isaiah 11:2, the Holy Spirit is declared to be "the Spirit of wisdom and understanding." He has power to impart divine wisdom and understanding to men. Thus is introduced the extensive doctrine of the teaching ministry of the Spirit (1 Cor. 2:12; 1 John 2:27; John 16:12-15). According to verse 18 and in the exercise of this ministry, the eyes of the heart, not the understanding merely, are to be enlightened. When revealed by the Spirit, the deep things of God are not addressed to the human understanding alone; they claim the response of the affections and will.

These divinely imparted themes include the heavenly blessings which have occupied the opening portion of this Epistle, the present effectual call of each child of God into the prospect of soon sharing the glory of Christ's resurrection, and the riches of the glory of His inheritance in the saints (verse 19). It would be profitable to dwell on these riches of grace and glory as disclosed in other portions of the Word of God where they will be seen to appear and reappear, especially in the Gospel by John and in the Epistles of the New Testament.

Likewise the divinely enabled heart will comprehend "the exceeding greatness of his power to us-ward who believe."

Standards of Divine Power

Three standards of divine power are set forth in the Scriptures. First, in the past dispensation the evidence of Jehovah's power, oft cited, was His deliverance of Israel out of Egypt. "I, Jehovah, which brought you out of the land of Egypt." Second, divine power will be measured in the future dispensation of Israel's kingdom glory in the earth by the yet future regathering of that nation from all countries into their own land. Thus we read in Jeremiah 23:7, 8:"Therefore, behold, the days come, saith the Lord, that they shall no more say, The Lord liveth which brought up the children of Israel out of the land of Egypt; but, The Lord liveth which brought up and which led the seed of the house of Israel out of the north country, and from all countries whither I had driven them; and they shall dwell in their own land."

That this final gathering of Israel into their own land is a miracle wrought by divine power is revealed in Matthew 24:31. This elect nation is to be assembled under the ministrations of the angels. Third, over against all this, and in contrast to it, the standard of divine power in this age is "his mighty power, which he wrought in Christ, when he raised him from the dead, and set him at his own right hand in the heavenly places, far above all principality, and power, and might, and dominion, and every name that is named, not only in this world, but also in that which is to come: and hath put all things under his feet, and gave him to be head over all things to the church, which is his body, the fulness of him that filleth all in all" (verses 19-23).

In considering the order of events in the resurrection and

exaltation of Christ as here stated, it should be remembered that all that is set forth in this description is stated primarily to the end that the believer may be properly impressed with the *greatness* of the power—the same power which wrought in Christ—which is engaged to accomplish for him everything that God has purposed, according to His election, predestination, and sovereign adoption. True, the Redeemer and His redemption will be provided, as well as the enabling power to believe; but, beyond these issues which are within the boundaries of time, the divine, eternal purpose will yet be realized to its full fruition, and is certain because of the "*exceeding greatness of the power*" which is engaged to that end. Nor should it be forgotten that all this disclosure is but a part of the Apostle's oft-repeated prayer wherein he makes request that, through the teaching work of the Spirit, these marvels which demonstrate the divine sufficiency might be comprehended by those who are the objects of these riches of grace and glory. Often in the Scriptures does the Spirit of God bring to our attention the certainty of all things which God has purposed, and happy indeed is the one who, by divine illumination, enters into the heart-understanding of these things.

But what, after all, is the measure of this exceeding great power which is to us-ward who believe? The record of it is given for our understanding—if so be that we are taught of the Spirit. Second only in importance is this theme to that of election and predestination with which the Epistle opened. What God has purposed He will realize, and to an absolute degree. What He has begun He will complete with that perfection which belongs to Infinity. This exceeding great power which is to us-ward who believe has already been manifested in four ways in behalf of Christ:

First, *Christ was raised from the dead*, not from a dormant state, as is suggested by the usual illustrations of resurrection which men employ, such as the lily bulb, the cocoon, and the egg, but from the estate of *death*. From this estate He was raised to a sphere far above that which He occupied on the earth before His death. The resurrection of Christ is more than the reversal of His death; and more, indeed, than a restoration such as characterized all previous so-called resurrections. Christ became a new order of Being. The Second Person of the Trinity was always present in Christ from the moment of His gestation in the virgin's womb to His exaltation in glory; but His humanity presented ever-changing aspects. As a child, He "grew and waxed strong in spirit." He who was "from everlasting to ever-lasting" came to be "thirty years of age"; and that body which was mortal, being subject to death, became immortal and He who was dead is now alive forever more. He who alone has immortality (1 Tim. 6:16) is now the first-fruits of resurrection—the only present representation in glory of that host of redeemed ones who will soon be with Him and be like Him.

Every power of Satan and man had combined to retain Christ's body in the tomb. The keys of death were apparently in Satan's hands until the resurrection of Christ (cf. Heb. 2:14 with Rev. 1:18). The greatest earthly power had set its seal upon the tomb, and none could loose the "pains of death" (Acts 2:24) other than God. Though, in the mystery of the Trinity, it is declared that Christ came forth from the tomb by His own will and power (John 2:19; 10:17, 18) and that He was quickened by the Spirit (1 Pet. 3:18), it is stated upwards of twenty-five times that Christ was raised by the power of God the Father. Thus, in this passage (verse 20) it is revealed that the resurrection was due to the exercise of the Father's mighty power which "he wrought in Christ when he raised him from the dead." This same mighty power, we are assured, is not only engaged to raise the believer from the dead, but is engaged to accomplish all that has been divinely predetermined for him unto eternal glory.

Second, *the Ascension of Christ* is a measurement of divine power to us-ward who believe. Though directly presented but three times (Mark 16:19; Luke 24:49-52; Acts 1:9), the ascension of Christ is often referred to in the Acts and Epistles as an important aspect of divine power (Acts 2:33; 3:21; 5:31; 7:55; Rom. 8:34; Phil. 2:9; 3:20; Col. 3:1; 1 Thess. 1:10; 4:16; 2 Thess. 1:7; Heb. 1:3; 1 Pet. 3:22; Rev. 3:21).

This body of truth, which is of great importance as evidence of the ascension and present position of Christ, is introduced at this point in the Ephesian letter as a ground of confidence that what God has purposed for the believer He is abundantly able to accomplish.

The present exaltation of Christ to a sphere far above all principalities and powers is a theme which transcends the range of unaided human understanding. The Spirit alone can impress the heart with that revelation which is here intended to create assurance in the child of God that he will himself realize all that God has purposed for him. This purpose includes no less than a partaking with Christ of that exalted glory. Of His own, Christ said, "Where I am, there ye shall be also," and, "The glory which thou gavest me I have given them."

Third, "*And hath put all things under his feet.*" It was in this same connection that Christ said, "All power is given unto me in heaven and on earth" (Matt. 28:18; cf. Luke 4:5, 6), and by Him shall all things be subdued (1 Cor. 15:25, 26). Great, indeed, is the power to us-ward who believe; for we are destined to reign with Christ and share with Him His authority. The Christian experiences little of the exercise of this authority now. At the present time he shares the rejection of his Lord; for all who will live godly shall suffer persecution (2 Tim. 3:12).

Fourth, "*And gave him to be head over all things to the church.*" Returning thus at the close of the first chapter to the subject which was in view at the beginning, the Apostle makes mention of that group of humanity which, because called out from both Jews and Gentiles into a heavenly association in Christ, is properly called an *ekklesia*, or Church. The fact which is uppermost here is that Christ, by divine appointment and power, is now Head over all things to the Church. The term Head combines two important aspects of truth: (1) Christ now presides over the Church as the One who directs every moment of life and every act of service of those who comprise this heavenly company. He is the bestower of gifts (4:8), and, by the Spirit, directs the exercise of those gifts (1 Cor. 12:4-7). (2) But Christ is now Head over the Church in the sense that from Him she draws all spiritual vitality. Because He lives, the members of His body live also. He is to the Church as the vine is to the branches, as the shepherd is to the sheep, as the corner-stone is to the building, and as the bridegroom is to the bride.

The Benefit of Believing

Special attention should be given to the fact that all the stupendous benefits enumerated in the first Chapter of the Ephesian letter are, on the human side, secured upon the one condition of believing. It is stated that the power of God is to us-ward who believe. In accordance with the plan of salvation by divine grace, no other condition could be imposed. Not only does God undertake all this measureless benefit, but the very faith by which it is received is itself a gift of God.

Section Six

Ephesians 2:1-3

1 And you hath he quickened, who were dead in trespasses and sins;
2 Wherein in time past ye walked according to the course of this world, according to the prince of the power of the air, the spirit that now worketh in the children of disobedience:
3 Among whom also we all had our conversation in times past in the lusts of our flesh, fulfilling the desires of the flesh and of the mind; and were by nature the children of wrath, even others.

At the opening of Chapter 2, the Apostle descends again from the contemplation of those exalted heights of heavenly position and glory which are accorded to the Church, constituting her spiritual blessings in the heavenly association in Christ, to the level of that estate which all the unsaved now occupy and from which each and every child of God has been saved. No new theme is introduced. In the first Chapter it has been disclosed that God is Sovereign over all things and all that is wrought by Him is wrought after the counsel of His own will. Likewise it is revealed that His limitless power has had its demonstration in the resurrection and exaltation of Christ, and that the resurrection and exaltation of Christ is an assurance to all who believe that, because of the fact that His mighty power is now engaged in their behalf, no purpose of God for them can ever fail. At the beginning of Chapter 2, the sovereign, eternal purpose of God is still in view, though for the moment the text is concerned with but one detail of that purpose—the manifestation of measureless grace in the salvation of men.

The Greatness of His Grace

The purpose of God incorporates vastly more than the mere rescue of sinners from their doom, as wonderful as that rescue is. God is the Designer and Creator of all things; His preservation is extended to all things; and His providence is guiding all things in order that, agreeable to His own sovereign will, all things may redound to the praise of His glory and grace. To this end sin is permitted its manifestation in the universe—first in heaven, and then upon the earth; a race is allowed to fall; a Savior is provided who by His death and resurrection declares to an infinite degree the love and grace of God; and the individual sinner, according to divine election, is called and saved unto an eternal heavenly glory.

One all-inclusive decree extending in its scope from eternity to eternity and wrought throughout on the plane of Infinity must, of necessity, present unsolvable mysteries to a finite mind—the permission and manifestation of evil, the advent and sacrifice of the Savior, and the choice of an elect company which through all eternity is to be a demonstration to all created intelligences of the marvels of divine grace. Nevertheless, the revelation of this divine program is made, and is to be *believed*, even though in all its parts it cannot be understood by the mind of man.

However free God may have been in the forming of His all-inclusive plan, we are assured that, having determined upon a plan, He is now bound by the laws of His own unchangeable character to execute that plan to infinite perfection. Thus necessities are confronted and limitations are imposed which are to be respected and observed both by God and man. On the divine side, a Savior must be provided; for there could be no salvation of the lost apart from the incarnation, death, and resurrection of the Son of God.

According to the original divine arrangement, a blood-shedding sacrifice is a necessity as immutable in its nature as the character of God. Man did not originate the situation expressed by the words, "Without shedding of blood, there is no remission" but God, having so decreed, could not, consistently, deviate from this demand. Again, by the divine arrangement it is originally decreed that there shall be no salvation for men apart from a personal faith in the saving power of God, and there could be no variation in the execution of this requirement. It is imperative, therefore, when descending in thought from the original, all-inclusive purpose of God to the detail of the salvation of a sinner, to recognize the immutability of every aspect of the divine purpose.

Of the many transforming blessings which are wrought of God for the sinner at the moment of believing, there is one which, according to its emphasis in the New Testament, is of primary importance. The second chapter of Ephesians opens with the words, "And you hath he quickened [made alive] who were dead in trespasses and sins." In the original Greek the construction is incomplete at this point, being more precisely re-stated in verse 5: "Even when we were dead in sins, hath quickened [made alive] us together with Christ." The change from the use of "you" to "we" in these verses is significant, indicating, as it does, that this transforming blessing is for Jew and Gentile alike. Likewise, the fact that the verb is in a tense which denotes a transaction completed at some moment in the past, is of doctrinal importance; for by one act of sovereign, saving power, *all* who have believed were, at the moment of believing, made alive with Christ. No subsequent achievement is implied. This fundamental aspect of salvation is both instantaneous and complete in its character.

To have been "made alive with Christ" is an experience which is no less than the reception of and sharing in His resurrection life. The reception of Christ's resurrection life in conjunction with the baptism with the Spirit by which the believer is joined to the Lord, constitutes the entrance into the far-reaching realities of the New Creation. Though shrouded in mystery, the fact remains that to have partaken of the divine nature is to have been "joined to the Lord," and to have been "joined to the Lord" is to have partaken not only of the divine nature, but to have shared legitimately and eternally in all the fellowship, achievement, and glory of the Triune God. To Jew and Gentile alike the gospel invitation is now addressed, and, by those who believe, the saving power of God is experienced. Measureless, indeed, is this divine power! It is none other than "the working of his mighty power which he wrought in Christ when he raised him from the dead and set him at his own right hand in the heavenly"; and significant, indeed, in this connection, is the statement found in verse 6: "And hath raised us up together, and made us sit together in the heavenly in Christ Jesus."

The essential fact, then, that believers are now "made alive with Christ" involves no less a reality than that they are now sharing in the position and exaltation of the resurrected, glorified Christ. But of these heavenly blessings in Christ, more will be seen in later portions of this Epistle.

There are two aspects of the gospel appeal: the invitation is both *away from* the lost estate, and *unto* a heavenly position and glory. Christ emphasized this two-fold fact when He said that the one who believes on Him "should not perish, but have everlasting life" (John 3:16; 10:28). Both of these aspects of truth are present in Ephesians 2:1-3; though, in this passage, the emphasis falls on that lost condition from which all who believe on Christ have been saved. In verse 12, record is given of the universal position of the Gentiles as being without God and without hope; but in verses 2 and 3, the present condition of all—both Jew and Gentile—who are out of Christ is disclosed. There are national promises for Israel which can never be broken, and there are prophecies of a coming, earthly glory for the Gentiles.

But in the present dispensation, in which God is dealing only with individuals on the basis of their faith in Christ, there is no difference between the unregenerate Jew and the unregenerate Gentile; both are now helpless and hopeless apart from the grace of God as it is in Christ (Rom. 3:9; 10:12). The present standing of the unregenerate—both Jew and Gentile—is precisely stated in Romans 1:18-32; 3:10-20, which passages, along with Ephesians 4:17-19, may well be considered in connection with Ephesians 2:2, 3; for it is of vital importance to those who would know God's saving grace that they comprehend, as well, the present condition of those who are lost.

As but one feature of the estate of the saved is mentioned in Ephesians 2:1-3, out of the many revealed elsewhere in the Scriptures, so, likewise, but four features of the estate of the lost, out of the many, are here recorded.

They are dead in trespasses and sins.

Just as the imparted life, mentioned in verse 1, is a life from God and therefore never to be confused with mere human life (much less a manner of living), so, in like manner, a deeper aspect of sin than that of a habit or practice of sinning is here declared. The charge brought forward in this passage is not that men commit sin, which accusation few would deny; it is rather the more serious charge that men are *dead* in sin. That is, they are in the state of spiritual death which is caused by sin, and, because they are in that state, they can produce nothing but sin.

The true relationship between sin and death will be discovered only from the Word of God. The fundamental character of sin may be defined as any transgression of, or want of conformity to, the character of God. All the present important classifications of sin—*imputed* sin, *imparted* sin, *personal* sin, and the *judicial reckoning* under sin—are traceable directly to the original act of sin on the part of the first sinner. Sin in its every form is exceedingly sinful, and that because of the fact that it is contrary to the character of God. His character is the touchstone for all motive and conduct whether in heaven or on the earth. The first sin, it is revealed, was committed as an act of willfulness on the part of the highest of all created intelligences in heaven. His moral degradation followed (Isa. 14:12-14). The same angelic being imported sin into the earth at the time when he persuaded Adam and Eve to pursue a similar course of willful disobedience toward God. In the latter instance and according to the divine warning, death followed—spiritual death on the same day, with both physical death and the second death following in unavoidable sequence.

Not only did these three forms of death become the inheritance of Adam, but they, of necessity, became the portion of his posterity; for Adam, whose nature and constitution had descended to the level of a fallen creature, was able, following his fall, to generate only "after his kind." His posterity, each and every individual, is born into a state of spiritual death from which there could be no rescue apart from the quickening, regenerating power of the Spirit of God. Adam, having died spiritually, generated a race that is spiritually dead, both because of the inflexible law of heredity, and because of their share in the sin of their federal head, being as they were, in the loins of their father Adam when he sinned (cf. Heb. 7:9, 10). Innocent infants need redemption, and those infants who die, we are assured, are redeemed, but not on the ground of their innocence; their redemption being on the ground of the grace of God which is exercised toward sinners for whom Christ has died. Every member of Adam's race, it is revealed, is born into the world in a state which is described as "dead in trespasses and sins."

They are walking according to the course of this world.

That spiritual death rather than physical death is in view is proven by the statement that those who are here said to be *dead*, are, nevertheless, "walking according to the course of this world." This world is their sphere since it answers every requirement of their fallen natures. No more illuminating description of the walk, which is according to this world, is found than that recorded in verse three: "Among whom also we all had our conversation [manner of life] in times past in the lusts of our flesh, fulfilling the desires of the flesh and of the mind." Spiritual death is a separation of soul and spirit from God and is the common heritage of all, unless, through divine grace, they experience regeneration by the Spirit of God.

They are walking according to the prince of the power of the air.

Reference is made in this Scripture to Satan, who is also "the god of this world" (2 Cor. 4:4), "the prince of this world" (John 16:11), and, according to this passage, the one who is in control over the lives of all who are unregenerate. The disobedience to which reference is made is not personal, but collective; for "by one man's disobedience many were made sinners." Similarly, the doctrinal designation, "children of obedience," does not imply personal obedience, but refers rather to the fact that "by the obedience of one shall many be made righteous" (Rom. 5:19). Thus it is declared that each unregenerate person is a "child of disobedience" and is therefore one in whom Satan is now "working" (literally, energizing). Satan is not said to be energizing a limited class who are notoriously evil; he is energizing each and every unregenerate person. In like manner, each and every regenerate person is now energized by God (Phil. 2:13).

They are by nature the children of wrath.

The Apostle, a Jew, while addressing Gentiles, includes himself by the words "we all" (verse 3). Fallen humanity in its vanity desires ever to "make a fair show in the flesh," and they "comparing themselves with themselves are not wise." Regardless of the opinion of men, it is true that all—the most zealous legalist, along with the meritless, whether Jew or Gentile—are "under sin," "dead in trespasses and sins," and "the children of wrath." Hope is never discovered within the range of human virtue or merit. All such confidence is excluded. The fruit cannot be accepted when the tree and its roots are condemned. Only a merciful God can save those who are otherwise so hopelessly lost, and to the mercy of God the Apostle now turns with boundless confidence.

Section Seven
Ephesians 2:4-10

4   But God, who is rich in mercy, for his great love wherewith he loved us,

5   Even when we were dead in sins, hath quickened us together with Christ, (by grace ye are saved;)

6   And hath raised us up together, and made us sit together in heavenly places in Christ Jesus:

7   That in the ages to come he might shew the exceeding riches of his grace, in his kindness toward us through Christ Jesus,

8   For by grace are ye saved through faith; and that not of yourselves: it is the gift of God:

9   Not of works, lest any man should boast.

10 For we are his workmanship, created in Christ Jesus unto good works, which God hath before ordained that we should walk in them.

Over against the dark picture of human ruin presented in Ephesians 2:1-3, the Apostle now proceeds in verses 4 to 10 to set forth the only existing hope for man, namely, the fact that God is "rich in mercy for his great love wherewith he loved us, even when we were dead in sins." With full recognition of the depths to which man has fallen, it is nevertheless declared that there is abundant salvation for all who *believe*: a salvation which so far exceeds the ruin that it not only reverses all that man lost by the fall, but it lifts him up far above his original unfallen state to the highest conceivable position in heaven, there to share forever the fellowship and the glory of the Triune God. Reference at this point to the divine mercy is not a recognition of an immediate compassion which might be supposed to have been engendered in the heart of God upon His discovery that, through some unforeseen accident, man had fallen from the high estate in which he was created to the lowest depths of depravity; it is rather a reference to that compassion which abides eternally in the very nature of God. Divine mercy antedates the fall of man to the same degree to which God Himself antedates man. In fact the Scriptures clearly indicate (Eph. 2:7; Rom. 11:32; Gal. 3:22) that the sin and ruin of man was permitted, in part, to the end that the eternal mercy of God might be manifested. Certainly the tragedy of sin did not engender a compassion in the heart of God which before was foreign to Him.

His Great Mercy

There is a threefold, present and immediate exercise of divine mercy. First, God is said to be merciful to those who put their trust in Him. To them He is "the Father of mercies" (2 Cor. 1:3), and they are invited to draw near to His throne of grace where, they are assured, they will now "obtain mercy" (Heb. 4:16). Second, the divine mercy will yet be manifested in behalf of Israel when they are regathered into their own land (Isa. 54:7). Third, mercy is exercised, also, when the individual sinner is called from his lost estate and saved by the grace of God (Rom. 9:15, 18; 1 Tim. 1:13). However, the mercy of God has had its supreme manifestation in the giving of His Son for the lost of this world. Sinners who believe are not now said to be saved through the immediate and personal exercise of divine mercy; but rather, since the mercy of God has provided a Savior who is the perfect Substitute for them, both as a sin-bearer, that they might be forgiven all trespasses, and as the righteous ground of a complete justification, God is said to be "just" when He justifies the one who does no more than to "believe in Jesus" (Rom. 3:26). Thus, from every angle of approach, God is seen to be "rich in mercy."

Of the immediate spiritual blessings which are wrought for the individual at the moment he believes, some are to be classified as *possessions*, and some as *positions*. Likewise some are wrought *in* him, and some are wrought *for* him. These distinctions occur in verses 5 and 6, where, it will be observed, the believer is first seen to be the recipient of divine life, which is a possession and a blessing wrought *in* him. He is in like manner raised and seated in the heavenly in Christ Jesus, which is a new position and a blessing wrought for him. Thus the Apostle cites two of the many immediate spiritual blessings which accompany salvation as representative of all that enters into the gracious saving work of God—one belonging to the new *possessions* and the other belonging to the new *positions*—and it is obvious that in each case he has selected that blessing which is supreme within the group to which it belongs.

The first of these spiritual blessings—the impartation of divine life—has been considered in the previous article in an exposition of Chapter 2, verse 1, which passage records the first mention in this Epistle of the fact that divine life is imparted. The second blessing, now to be considered—that of being raised and seated with Christ (verse 6)—provides and secures, for the one who trusts in the Savior, absolute identity with the risen Christ and eternal glory with Him forever.

Both as to resurrection and as to seating in the heavenly, the believer is now vitally joined to Christ. The word *together*, twice used in this verse, relates him, not to the fellowship of the saints as in 1 Thessalonians 4:17, but to the risen and glorified Christ. The Apostle is justified in the confidence that the reader will not have forgotten the setting forth of Christ's glorious resurrection and exaltation in the verses immediately preceding (1:20-23), and that he will understand to some degree the surpassing, heavenly reality and glory which belong to the one who, because of his union with Christ, is now raised and seated *in Christ Jesus*, far above all earthly or heavenly comparison (1:21).

To be *in Christ*, which is the portion of all who are saved, is to partake of all that Christ has done, all that He is, and all that He will ever be. It is to have died in His death, to have been buried in His burial, to have been raised in His resurrection, to have ascended in His ascension, and to be seated now *with Him* (because he is *in* Him) in glory. Such is the believer's present position in Christ Jesus.

Over against all this, and in no way to be confused with it, is the experimental fact that a bodily resurrection and actual heavenly exaltation await all those who "sleep in Jesus"; and a bodily translation and heavenly exaltation await all who are "alive and remain unto the coming of the Lord"; the present, unalterable fact of the believer's position in Christ being the guarantee of the yet future experience. A parallel description of this coming glory is found in Colossians 3:1-4. "If ye then be risen with Christ, seek those things which are above, where Christ sitteth on the right hand of God. Set your affection on things above, not on things on the earth. For ye are dead [ye died], and your life is hid with Christ in God. When Christ, who is our life, shall appear, then shall ye also appear with him in glory." And Christ has declared, "Because I live, ye shall live also" (John 14:19). That this salvation far exceeds the ruin of sin is seen in the fact that by sin man fell from the level of fellowship with his Creator on the earth; but by saving grace he is exalted to fellowship with God in heaven. The probationary life in Adam was precarious and insecure; but the child of God has a new life imparted, which is Christ in him, and which is in no way related to that Adamic life which was ruined through sin. The life of Christ *imparted*, like the merit of Christ *imputed*, is held on no probationary condition, but is the free and unalterable gift of God to all who *believe*.

In verses 7 and 10, the Apostle presents two of the three revealed motives which actuate the heart of God in the salvation of sinners. These three motives are here mentioned in an order beginning with that which, to human estimation, seems least important, and ending with that which seems most important.

His Workmanship

First, in verse 10 it is stated that, "We are his workmanship, created in Christ Jesus unto good works, which God hath before ordained that we should walk in them"; the divine objective being, according to this passage, that "good works" may result from that which is wrought of God, and that which is wrought of God is no less than a new "creation in Christ Jesus." Such is the result of "His workmanship." It is of interest to note here that in the Bible there is reference to "wicked works," or "works of darkness," to "dead works," and to "good works."

That "good works" do not include any and every good thing one might choose to do is indicated in this passage wherein it is asserted that these "works" are limited to the execution in one's life of those activities which "God hath before ordained that we should walk in them." In other words, reference is made by this designation to the life and service of the child of God who, being fully yielded to God, experiences the out-working of God's purpose in his life. It is the discovery of "that good, and acceptable, and perfect, will of God" (Rom. 12:2). Of a certainty, no "good works" will ever come from the life of an unregenerate person. For that reason and to the end that good works may be realized, God has been moved to the recreation of men in Christ Jesus. But, on the other hand, in the sight of God, how vitally important, according to the Scriptures, are these "good works!"

To be saved unto good works is a divine undertaking which should never be confused with the unscriptural notion that one might be saved *by* good works. In every aspect of it, "salvation is of the Lord"; but it is unto that manner of life which He has before ordained.

His Motive

Second, in John 3:16 it is revealed that the divine motive in saving men is, "that they might not perish but have everlasting life." Thus the compassion of God for those who are lost and doomed is declared. So great, indeed, is His compassion that He gave His Only Begotten Son to die in their room and stead, "the just for the unjust"; and it is not difficult to recognize how great a problem that sacrificial death solved for the One Who "so loved the world." The sinfulness of men could not be ignored by the Righteous One Whose character is outraged and Whose government is willfully opposed by their sins; but, on the other hand, He could, if He loved the offender sufficiently, provide a substitute to take the unalterable judgments which divine holiness must ever impose upon sin. This is precisely what God did. Christ as Substitute accomplished a *propitiation* toward God, a *reconciliation* toward the sinner, and a *redemption* toward sin. Great, indeed, are the benefits which accrue to the believer through the death of Christ that he "should not perish, but have everlasting life." However, it should be observed that all this has been wrought by God, not merely that human suffering may be relieved or glory experienced, but rather to the end that His compassion might be satisfied. It is all because of the fact that "God so loved the world." There is yet, nevertheless, a higher motive for the exercise of the saving power of God than His compassion for the lost, though that compassion be as boundless as Infinity itself.

His Objective

Third, it is declared in Ephesians 2:7, that God saves the lost with the objective in view "that in the ages to come he might show the exceeding riches of his grace in his kindness toward us through Christ Jesus." Thus it is disclosed that the supreme purpose of God in salvation is that His grace in all its "exceeding riches" might have an adequate manifestation. This is but a fuller statement of the declaration twice made at the beginning of this Epistle (verses 6,12) wherein it is revealed that the divine purpose to display the exceeding riches of His grace is according to His election and predestination, being one of the eternal purposes which He purposed in Christ Jesus. To this end, sin was permitted its manifestation, the Savior was provided, and the sinner is brought to the saving knowledge of Christ—all in the eternal purpose of God. Thus it will be recognized that the manifestation of the exceeding riches of grace indicates a divine motive which not only antedates the exercise of divine compassion as seen in the sacrificial death of Christ, but is itself that divine purpose which required Christ's sacrifice for its realization.

There was that in God which had never been expressed or manifested. His glory, His power, and His wisdom had been declared in some measure through creation; but His compassion for the lost, and all that is in His heart to do for those who are utterly doomed, had never been disclosed. It is not difficult to believe that the desire to exercise this essential part of His nature could not be suppressed forever, and that, when He undertook to demonstrate His infinite kindness toward His enemies, the manifestation would be on the plane of Infinity, and that it would be as perfect and worthy of Himself as are all the works of God.

A sharp distinction is properly drawn between the compassionate love of God for sinners, and His grace which is now offered to them in Christ Jesus. Divine love and divine grace are not one and the same. God might love sinners with an unutterable compassion and yet, because of the demands of outraged divine justice and holiness, be unable to rescue them from a righteous doom. However, as has been before stated, if love shall graciously provide for the sinner all that outraged justice and holiness could ever demand, the love of God would then be free to act without restraint in behalf of those for whom the perfect substitutionary sacrifice was made. This is Christ's achievement on the cross. On the other hand, divine grace in salvation is the unrestrained compassion of God acting toward the sinner on the basis of that freedom already secured through the righteous judgment against sin—secured by Christ in His sacrificial death. Divine love might desire to save, yet be unable righteously to do so; but divine grace is free to act since Christ has died. It is to be observed, then, that the eternal purpose of God is not the manifestation of His *love* alone, though His love and His mercy are, like His grace, mentioned in this context and expressed in Christ's death; but it is rather the manifestation of His *grace*.

The "exceeding riches of his grace" are no less than all that the infinite God can do for the sinner when every barrier is broken down and every moral hindrance is removed. The measureless character of "his kindness" toward the one who puts his trust in the Savior is seen in that transformation by which the sinner is taken from the lost estate and is exalted to the highest conceivable position in heaven, there to be "presented faultless" before the presence of God, "conformed to the image of his Son," and, "without blame before him" (1:4). What greater thing could infinite love desire than that the sinner utterly doomed on earth should be, through riches of grace, "like him" in heaven (1 John 3:2)?

His Salvation

God alone is able to accomplish the marvelous transformations which enter into the eternal salvation of the sinner. Therefore, it is reasonable to the highest degree, that He must reserve every feature of that transaction to Himself. On this aspect of truth, the Apostle declares (verses 8 and 9), that it is "by grace are ye saved," and "not of works lest any man should boast." Salvation is God's unrecompensed gift (John 10:28; Rom. 6:23), and therefore, although it is a thing in which the saved one may delight forever, he cannot boast as one who has added any feature to it. Even the faith by which it is received is itself a *gift* from God. As to this fact, each saved person will freely confess that he would not have turned to God had it not been for the drawing, calling and illuminating power of the Spirit. As to who will thus turn to God, God alone must determine; for we are chosen in Him before the foundation of the world (1:4). There is no after-thought with God. The Gospel is to be preached to every creature, and it is the divine responsibility, through that preaching, to execute the eternal purpose. This God has done, is doing, and will do to the end.

Section Eight

Ephesians 2:11-22

11 Wherefore remember, that ye being in time past Gentiles in the flesh, who are called Uncircumcision by that which is called the Circumcision in the flesh made by hands;

12 That at that time ye were without Christ, being aliens from the commonwealth of Israel, and strangers from the covenants of promise, having no hope, and without God in the world:

13 But now in Christ Jesus ye who sometimes were far off are made nigh by the blood of Christ.

14 For he is our peace, who hath made both one, and hath broken down the middle wall of partition between us;

15 Having abolished in his flesh the enmity, even the law of commandments, contained in ordinances; for to make in himself of twain one new man, so making peace;

16 And that he might reconcile both unto God in one body by the cross, having slain the enmity thereby:

17 And came and preached peace to you which were afar off, and to them that were nigh.

18 For through him we both have access by one Spirit unto the Father.

19 Now therefore ye are no more strangers and foreigners, but fellow-citizens, with the saints, and of the household of God;

20 And are built upon the foundation of the apostles and prophets, Jesus Christ himself being the chief corner stone;

21 In whom all the building fitly framed together groweth unto a holy temple in the Lord:

22 In whom ye also are builded together for an habitation of God through the Spirit.

At the beginning of this section of the Epistle (2:11-22), the Apostle again reminds the Ephesian believers of their former estate from which they were saved—a most commendable consideration, indeed, for all children of God in any generation, and an exercise of mind which the Apostle himself often experienced. The problem of human depravity and failure is never solved by any plan or process which makes light of sin, or which underestimates the lost estate of man. It is rather solved by the discovery of the marvels of divine grace in Christ Jesus by Whom every need of a lost soul is perfectly met. There is slight need of a Savior if we are not wholly lost apart from Him. But, on the other hand, having acknowledged the hopeless condition in which grace found us, there is occasion for unceasing thanksgiving to Him Who saves to the uttermost.

In this section we are reminded of the original distinction between Jew and Gentile and here, also, the present union of these two lines of human life in Christ Jesus is set forth. The disclosure of the fact concerning the union between Jews and Gentiles forms the third major revelation in this Epistle regarding this heavenly people. First, at the opening of Chapter 1, the Church is described as to her exalted position and heavenly blessing *in Christ*—predestined, as she was, before the foundation of the world. Second, at the close of the same Chapter, the Church is seen as that glorious company over which the risen and glorified Christ is now Head and which, in turn, is "the fulness of him that filleth all in all." Third, while in the portion of the Epistle thus far considered, much important truth is added as to the purpose and grace of God toward the individual who believes, the section now under contemplation presents particularly the fact that the corporate Church is composed of a union of both Jews and Gentiles.

The Circumcision

The Jewish seal of circumcision forms the basis of distinction between the two branches of the human family. No doubt the Apostle from childhood had been familiar with this terminology which he here employs. He distinguishes the Jew as "the Circumcision" and the Gentile as "the Uncircumcision," and this circumcision referred to is that which is physical, typical, and wrought by hands; and it is a foreshadowing of the anti-typical, spiritual circumcision which belongs to one and all who are *in Christ*. Thus the Apostle recognizes again the present threefold classification of the human family: the Uncircumcision, the Circumcision made by hands (2:11), and the Circumcision made without hands (Col. 2:11). However, the immediate contrast is between the Gentile and the Jew, or "the Uncircumcision" and "the Circumcision made by hands."

After nearly two thousand years in which the privileges that constitute the distinction between Gentile and Jew have been divinely set aside, it is difficult in the present time for one to realize the difference which prevailed between these two peoples at the beginning of the present age. Two underlying facts should be observed: first, God, while not releasing His power and sovereignty over the nations, had, nevertheless, declared His favor toward Israel alone, which people formed the acknowledged heritage of God. True, there was a welcome accorded to strangers who chose to ally themselves with Israel, but all were strangers who were not of Israel. There was no other nation or people who were the chosen of Jehovah (Deut. 7:6-11), to whom He was married (Jer. 3:14), whom alone He knew among the families of the earth (Amos 3:2), and whom He had redeemed from Egypt both by blood and by power (2 Sam. 7:23). Probably no passage of Scripture describes the peculiar estate of Israel before God more completely than Romans 9:4, 5. We read, "Who are Israelites; to whom pertaineth the adoption, and the glory, and the covenants, and the giving of the law, and the service of God, and the promises; whose are the fathers, and of whom as concerning the flesh Christ came, who is over all, God blessed forever. Amen."

Certainly Israel would have been reprehensible had she failed to acknowledge, or to respond to, this divine election. However, the distinction was national and provided no basis for that Pharisaism which came to prevail in the attitude of the Jews toward individual Gentiles.

Second, the prejudice of the Jew toward the Gentile, based upon divine favor, had come to be nothing less than hatred and contempt. To the Jew the Gentile was a "dog," and it was contrary to custom for a Jew to speak to a Gentile, let alone enter his house. Only divine command could persuade Peter to enter the house of Cornelius (Acts 10:20).

Probably no other Scripture describes the actual estate of the Gentile before God more completely than Ephesians 2:12. While the lost estate of the individual has been disclosed in verses 1 to 3 of this Chapter, the national position of the Gentile, which was really true of the individual, is described in verse 12. We read: "That at that time ye were without Christ, being aliens from the commonwealth of Israel, and strangers from the covenants of promise, having no hope, and without God in the world."

Six disqualifying charges are here preferred. The Gentiles were "without Christ," not only personally Christless, as all unsaved are, but having no national Messianic hope; they were outside Israel's one divinely recognized commonwealth; they were "strangers from the covenants of promise." This does not deny but what God had predicted great earthly blessings for the Gentiles in the coming Kingdom Age (Dan. 7:13, 14; Micah 4:2); it asserts, rather, that He had entered into no covenant with them as He had with Israel: the Gentiles had "no hope" since no covenant promise had been accorded them; and they were without God in the world. They could make no claim to His purpose or favor, and they formed that portion of humanity which was under the curse and was doomed to destruction. The world today knows little of the godless and hopeless condition of human life among the Gentiles in the days to which reference is made. We are told that, at the highest state of Greek culture under Alexander the Great, it was commonly held that the best thing was not to be born at all, and next to that was to die; so fully did the experience of the human heart reflect the actual relation which is unknowingly sustained to God.

A New Divine Purpose

In the midst of these distinctions between Jew and Gentile which were set up by God, owned of God, and accentuated by human prejudice and hatred, a new divine purpose was introduced; made possible on the ground of the death and resurrection of Christ and the advent of the Spirit on the day of Pentecost. That divine purpose is no less than the forming of a new body of heavenly people drawn from both Jews and Gentiles, each individual in that body perfected in Christ, and whole company to be to "the praise of the glory of his grace." Therefore, because it is to the glory of His grace, each individual in this company, whether Jew or Gentile, is called and saved upon that distinct principle of selection—the sovereign grace of God, apart from all human merit.

As a basis for this exercise of sovereign grace apart from human merit, the most startling divine decree was announced; startling, indeed, because never before heard of in the world, and because it is so contrary to the hitherto divinely sanctioned exaltation of Israel over the Gentiles. That decree declares that now there is "no difference" between Jew and Gentile: they are all *under sin* (Rom. 3:9). So, again, there is "no difference" between Jew and Gentile "for the same Lord over all is rich unto all that call upon him" (Rom. 10:12). According to the first declaration, the former distinction between Jews and Gentiles disappears by the fact that both classes are now, regardless of former relationships to Jehovah, *"under sin"* (*cf.* Gen. 3:22). According to the second declaration, the way into this highest heavenly glory is open to all who will believe. The estate *"under sin"* consists in the fact that God now refuses to accept any human merit, national or personal, as a credit or contribution toward that salvation which is offered the individual in and through Christ.

God thus strips each human being of all hope in himself and shuts him up to that perfect salvation alone which is in Christ and which provides the eternal and infinite perfection of Christ. It might seem unkind to take away what little merit one might be supposed to have before God, but in the end it is not unkind. It is rather, "that he might have mercy upon all" (Rom. 11:32). The grace of God is not a thing which adjusts itself to the greater or less degree of human merit, it is a *standard* whole; that is, since all merit is excluded, it requires the same degree of grace to save one individual as it does to save another. And the result is not to the glory of man to the slightest degree: rather, it is all to the praise of the glory of His grace (1:6; 2:7-9). There was little for the Gentile to unlearn in connection with this new age-purpose and plan of salvation. He had no ground for hope before, and the Gospel of salvation by grace became to him as life from the dead. But the Jew stumbled over the way of salvation through the cross, and only a few, though their national preference is set aside for this age (Rom. 11:1-36), have been able to abandon their assumed national standing with God and to accept the exceeding grace of God in Christ.

This somewhat lengthy re-statement of the present ground of salvation by grace for Jew and Gentile alike may clarify the verses which follow in this context.

A New Position

By the words *"but now"* at the beginning of verse 13, a sharp contrast is drawn between the former estate of these Ephesian Gentiles described in verse 12, and their new position *in Christ*. Here they are told that they, as Gentiles, who were at a previous time "far off" from God, were then, because of their new position *in Christ*, "made nigh," not by external ordinances or human virtue, but by the blood of Christ. To be *nigh to God* is one of the exalted positions into which each believer is brought at the moment he is saved. The perfection of this position is seen from the fact that one could not be nearer to God in time or eternity than he is when *in Christ*. So perfect is the efficacy of the blood of Christ in providing a righteous ground for divine grace that every desire on the part of God, though prompted by infinite love, can now be satisfied completely in behalf of those who believe on Christ!

Verse 13 is closely related to verse 17 (*cf.* Isa. 59:17). In the former, only Gentiles are in view; but in the latter, both Jews and Gentiles are seen. The Gentiles are identified as those who, because of no former covenant relation to God, were "far off," while the Jews, because of their covenants, were "nigh"; but not nigh to the same degree in which the saved Jew and the saved Gentile are now, being *in* Christ and redeemed through His precious blood.

This new *position in Christ*, similar to other positions in Christ, has its corresponding *experience* in life. James said, "Draw nigh to God and he will draw nigh to you" (4:8). However, the *experimental* aspect, which depends on human adjustment and yieldedness to God, does not bear any relation to the new *position in Christ*, which position depends only upon the eternal, immutable merit of Christ.

In verse 14, Christ is declared to be "our peace"' and to have broken down the middle wall of partition between Gentile and Jew. The wall of separation, here said to be broken down, was set up by divine arrangement at the time when God entered into covenant relation with Abraham; but now a new thing is introduced ("new" as a declared testimony and actual undertaking, but, in purpose and promise, it is older than the created universe— *cf.* 1:4). By saving both Jew and Gentile alike, upon the same condition, and into the same heavenly glory, Christ becomes in the fullest sense their Peace; and, by reconciling both to God, becomes thereby the most effective of reconciling agencies.

Every distinction is lost in this glorious oneness *in Christ*. Neither Jew nor Gentile can rightfully claim superiority over the other since they are both perfected forever *in Christ* (Heb. 10:14). So, likewise, in addition to the fact that Christ establishes perfect peace between Jews and Gentiles, they being united to Him by faith, He breaks down the middle wall of partition between them. The revelation that Jews were under divine legislation not imposed on Gentiles—a fact typified by the wall which separated the court of the Gentiles in the Temple from the restricted area reserved only for the Jews—became a wall of separation between these people. By the death of Christ, the wall was broken down. The Gentiles were not elevated to the level of Jewish privilege; but the Jew was lowered to the level of the hopeless Gentile, from which position either Jew or Gentile might be saved through grace alone into a heavenly position and glory. In His flesh, Christ abolished the enmity, "even the law of commandments" (verse 15), and every aspect of law which might seem to provide, because of its meritorious character, a basis of man's responsibility to God. Thus placing the child of God, whether Jew or Gentile, upon a new obligation; not of striving to establish merit, but rather of living in all devotion to Him Whose perfect merit is vouchsafed to all who believe. This new obligation is elsewhere termed "the law of Christ" (Gal. 6:2; *cf.* 1 Cor. 9:21).

A Partition Removed

The removal of both the enmity and the partition between Jew and Gentile is divinely accomplished through the creation of "one new man"; not by renewing individual men, but by forming one new Body—the Church—of which Christ is the Head. Thus, in the Church (verse 16), He reconciles both Jew and Gentile "unto God in one body by the cross, having slain the enmity thereby"; separated, as they were, by the different relationships they sustained to God.

It is through Christ (verse 8) that we both—Jew and Gentile—have access by one Spirit unto the Father. This declaration provides indisputable evidence that we now have peace; and how marvelous is that peace when it is the portion of those who were not only at enmity among themselves with a divinely established partition dividing them, but who were enemies of God (Rom. 5:9)!

We now approach (verses 19-22) the fourth major revelation concerning the Church, which revelation is that the Church is a building of living stones of which Christ is the Chief Corner Stone. However, before this truth is introduced, the Apostle reminds these believers from among the Gentiles that they are "no more strangers and foreigners [as it was asserted in verse 12 that they once were], but fellow-citizens with the saints and of the household of God—a blessing which, it should be observed, is as much higher than the commonwealth and covenant privileges of Israel as heaven is higher than the earth. Though once excluded from the earthly Jerusalem, the Gentiles are now come with a gracious welcome to the heavenly Jerusalem (Heb. 12:22-24), in which city, the unregenerate Jew, with all his national preference and title to earthly Jerusalem, is an alien.

A New Foundation

The phrase, "fellow-citizens with the saints," must be received in its restricted meaning as also the fact that this spiritual structure is built on "the foundation of the apostles and [New Testament] prophets." God has had His saints in all dispensations, but they of the past ages have not formed any part of the Church. Saints are sanctified ones set apart unto God. That New Testament saints are advanced to a higher position of standing than the Old Testament saints (though not necessarily to more faith and piety), is revealed in Hebrews 10:10, where we read: "We are sanctified through the offering of the body of Jesus Christ once for all." This sanctification, or sainthood, could not be realized until Christ died and rose again, for it is characterized by position *in Him*, which position could be accorded only to those who are by the Spirit united to the risen Christ. It is true that all saints of all the ages will be gathered eventually before God in a new heaven and a new earth (Heb. 11:38-40; 12:22-24); but the Old Testament saints were not part of the New Creation *in Christ*, nor were they builded upon the foundation of the apostles and New Testament prophets. The more extended consideration of the peculiar character of the Corner Stone and the foundation of this building which "groweth unto an holy temple in the Lord" is reserved for consideration along with the opening portion of the following section.

Section Nine

Ephesians 2:19 to 3:13

19 Now therefore ye are no more strangers and foreigners, but fellow-citizens with the saints, and of the household of God;

20 And are built upon the foundation of the apostles and prophets, Jesus Christ himself being the chief corner stone;

21 In whom all the building fitly framed together groweth unto an holy temple in the Lord:

22 In whom ye also are builded together for a habitation of God through the Spirit.

1 For this cause I Paul, the prisoner of Jesus Christ for you Gentiles,

2 If ye have heard of the dispensation of the grace of God which is given me to you-ward:

3 How that by revelation he made known unto me the mystery; (as I wrote afore in few words;

4 Whereby, when ye read, ye may understand my knowledge in the mystery of Christ,)

5 Which in other ages was not made known unto the sons of men, as it is now revealed unto his holy apostles and prophets by the Spirit;

6 That the Gentiles should be fellowheirs, and of the same body, and partakers of his promise in Christ by the gospel:

7 Whereof I was made a minister, according to the gift of the grace of God given unto me by the effectual working of his power.

8 Unto me, who am less than the least of all saints, is this grace given, that I should preach among the Gentiles the unsearchable riches of Christ;

9 And to make all men see what is the fellowship of the mystery,

81

which from the beginning of the world hath been hid in God, who created all things by Jesus Christ:

10 To the intent that now unto the principalities and power, in heavenly places might be known by the church the manifold wisdom of God,

11 According to the eternal purpose which he purposed in Christ Jesus our Lord;

12 In whom we have boldness and access with confidence by the faith of him.

13 Wherefore I desire that ye faint not at my tribulations for you, which is your glory.

The second Chapter of Ephesians closes with the presentation of the Church (the whole company of those who are saved in this age) using as an illustration the figure of a building which is now in the process of formation. It is declared that the Church, like a building, is being built upon the foundation of the apostles and New Testament prophets, Jesus Christ Himself being the chief Corner Stone. It is *in Him* that all the building is being fitly framed together and is thus "growing" into an holy temple *in the Lord. In Him* the separate and various members are being builded *together* for an habitation of God through the Spirit. During the past dispensation the habitation of God was the tabernacle, and later the temple—the earthly sanctuary or holy place made with hands (*cf.* Heb. 8:2; 9:1, 2, 24)—which, though held in antithesis to the heavenly sanctuary into which Christ has now entered, was, nevertheless, the type of the present spiritual habitation of God in a temple of living stones. Indeed, each stone in the present temple is itself an habitation of God through the Spirit (1 Cor. 3:16, 17; 6:19)—a marvelous disclosure belonging to that body of truth which contemplates the individual believer's present relation to the Spirit of God.

An Habitation of God

However, at this point the Apostle is not dwelling on the truth which concerns the individual believer, but rather on that which has to do with the corporate Body of Christ; and his declaration is that the Church, as it is now being formed in the world, is being builded as an habitation of God through the Spirit. Israel *had* a building in which God was pleased to dwell: the Church *is* a building in which God is pleased to dwell.

The figure of a building, with its corner, or capstone as a representation of the Church in her relation to Christ, is one of the seven figures employed in the New Testament to indicate the relation which exists between Christ and the Church; each one setting forth, as it does, its own particular aspect of the Church's vital union with Christ. This particular figure suggests the fact and location of God's dwelling place in the world in this age; the importance and interdependence of each and every stone in the building; the fact that it is in the process of making; and, that in relation to it, Christ is all in all. Of these various disclosures, the fact that the building is now in the process of making is perhaps more stressed in this passage than in any other. This is the age of the outcalling of the Church and, whether she be conceived of as a "flock" in relation to the Shepherd, the "branches" in relation to the Vine, a "kingdom of priests" in relation to the High Priest, a "new creation" in relation to the Last Adam, a "body" in relation to its Head, a "bride" in relation to the Bridegroom, or a "building" in relation to the Corner Stone, the thought of *development* is everywhere represented. The salvation of even one soul is a step forward toward the final consummation of the whole.

As to the statement here made (verse 20) that these Gentile saints are builded on the foundation of apostles and prophets, it should be recognized that while the apostle is wholly foreign to the old order, the Old Testament prophet, though in the main anticipating Christ's Messianic ministry to Israel, did nevertheless pre-announce the suffering Savior (Luke 24:25; Acts 3:18, 21, 24; 10:43; Rom. 16:26) but, in this instance, both because of the order in which these ministries are named, and because of the later references (3:5; 4:11) of which more will be stated presently, there can be no doubt but what the New Testament prophet is in view. The dominating ministry of the early church prophets in confirming the saints and in forming of sound doctrine cannot be questioned (Acts 15:32).

Before the figure of the growing building is introduced, these Gentile saints are reminded that they are "fellow-citizens with the saints and of the household of God" (verse 19). The citizenship here implied is that of the heavenly city into which blessed abode the saints of all dispensations will yet be gathered

(Heb. 12:22-24; Phil. 3:20). In every case they are God's sanctified ones, but not necessarily of the same body or building. The Old Testament saints were holy men because of the "good report" which by faith, they obtained (Heb. 11:39); but, since the manifestation of God's Holy One, saintship has acquired a distinctive character which could never have been before. Believers are now holy because Christ has become their Sanctification (Heb. 10:10; 1 Cor. 1:30). They are not perfected by a "good report," but by the eternal and infinite perfection of Christ, being *in Him*. True it is that there are many eternal blessings which all saints will share alike (Deut. 33:3), yet it is equally true that to the Church has been accorded the highest position; for of no other company could it be said that, being *in Christ*, they are "blessed with every spiritual blessing in the heavenly."

The Household of God

So, likewise, we are, along with the saints of other ages, of the household of God. The household, like the citizenship, is large indeed; and, though the fellowship will doubtless extend to all who enter the heavenly city, of no other group who enter therein, is it said that they are now raised and seated with Christ" in the highest position and glory of God, nor that they will be His bride in the ages to come to the glory of His grace.

At the opening of Chapter three, the apostle reverts to himself and is reminded to do so by the truth he is presenting. He is the divinely chosen Apostle to the Gentiles, and, therefore, is properly responsible to establish his apostolic authority in order that his message may be recognized as being from God; especially is the recognition of his authority called for in connection with the revelation given to him concerning the Church. As to his loyalty to his commission, he reminds these Gentile saints that he is in prison for their sakes.

A new age, with its peculiar Gentile privilege, has been ushered in by the death and resurrection of Christ and by the descent of the Spirit on the Day of Pentecost. Jewish prejudice has been aroused to the point of violence, and there can be no doubt but what Paul is recognized by the Jews as the promoter of this Gentile movement. It was the Jewish malice which placed the Apostle in bonds. In this connection it is well to remember that the present equality of gospel privilege for Jew and Gentile alike, though so axiomatic to this generation, was in Paul's day a startling innovation cutting squarely across the grain of previous divine revelation regarding the prominence and national election of Israel. The new order of privilege was revolutionary, and, if it was to be accepted, its human agent who announced it must possesss divine credentials.

In proof of the fact that he had divine authority for the apostolic message, the Apostle here (verses 2-13) inserts a parenthetical passage of immense importance; resuming again, at verse 14, the original channel of his thought. He states that he is chosen of God to receive and declare a revelation of world-transforming import. A message which reduced the favored Jew to the level of the outcast Gentile (Rom. 3:9; 10:12); which asserted the utter worthlessness of human merit to those who had been taught to depend on naught else; and which offered a new and higher privilege even to Gentiles than had been previously enjoyed by the exclusive seed of Abraham, must, as it did, stir the unrelenting enmity toward the man who, under God, proclaimed this message. Thus we observe that the revelation of this new divine order for a new age was given to Paul, as it is directly declared in the immediate text (verse 2), and this is confirmed by the obvious fact that against him, as against no other, the hatred of the Jew was directed.

What then is the precise scope and character of this jealousy-provoking message? The answer is given in verse 6. But before approaching this disclosure the Apostle asserts that this special revelation was given to him (*cf.* verses 7-9) and through him to other "holy apostles and prophets by the Spirit." The revelation had been received by him previous to the writing of this Epistle, and that revelation had become the accepted order in the minds of others who, like Paul, were set for the proclamation of the newly revealed message. It was not to Peter, James nor John, though pillars in the Church, but to Paul only, that this distinctive revelation came.

Two Revelations

As pointed out when considering Ephesians 1:9, two distinct

revelations were given to the Apostle Paul: the first, concerning salvation by grace alone through faith apart from human merit, and on the ground of the work and merit of Christ (Gal. 1:11, 12); and the second, as set forth in this immediate context. (No consideration need be given here to less emphasized experiences on the part of the Apostle as recorded in Acts 26:19 and 2 Cor. 12:1-4. Note also the promise of Acts 26:16.) These two major revelations together form that larger body of truth which the Apostle designates as "my gospel" (2 Tim. 2:8).

According to verse 5, this revelation is the unfolding of a mystery, or sacred secret, "which in other ages was not made known unto the sons of men, as it is now revealed unto his holy apostles and prophets by the Spirit." No better definition of a New Testament mystery will be found than that set forth in this context. A New Testament mystery is a truth hitherto withheld, or "hidden in God" (verse 9), but now revealed. The sum total of all the mysteries in the New Testament represents that entire body of added truth found in the New Testament which is unrevealed in the Old Testament. On the other hand the New Testament mystery is to be distinguished from the mystery of the cults of Babylon and Rome, whose secrets were sealed and held on penalty of death; while the New Testament mystery, when it is revealed, is to be declared to the ends of the earth (verse 9), and is restricted only to the extent of the limitation of the natural man (1 Cor. 2:14).

The general assertion, sometimes made, that these mysteries did not appear at all in the Old Testament should be modified. They are not there advanced in any clearness or fulness of revelation. However, certain New Testament mysteries are anticipated in Old Testament prophecy and type. That Israel is judicially blinded is declared in Romans 11:25 to be a *mystery*. Yet that blindness is clearly predicted in Isaiah 6:9, 10 (*cf.* John 12:40, 41). Similarly the Church is typified in at least seven of the marriage unions of the Old Testament; is seen as the anti-type fullfilment of four out of the seven Feasts of Jehovah; and as the assembly to which reference is made in Psalm 22:22 (*cf.* Heb. 2:12). All this, though so evidently anticipating the Church, is not an adequate revelation of the great divine age-purpose in the outcalling of the Body and Bride of Christ, nor of that distinctive fact which in this context is termed the "mystery."

If, for the previous bringing in of other divine purposes of an earthly nature, it were necessary to employ "holy men of God who spake as they were moved by the Holy Ghost" (2 Peter 1:21), how reasonable is the declaration that "holy apostles and prophets" were used of the Lord for the present bringing in of the revelation of the heavenly purpose! Under these conditions is anyone justified in the assumption that the New Testament apostles and prophets who spoke forth a later revelation were one whit less honored of God as media of divine truth than the "sons of God"—the "holy men of God"—who spoke forth the former revelation? Messiah's kingdom occupied the Old Testament prophets' vision. They saw not the mystery of that "New Man" (2:15) which bears collectively the name *Christ* (1 Cor. 12:12). True, indeed, the Messiah was to die a sacrificial death. This fact had not only been typified, but it had been solemnly promised in every Jewish sacrifice. On the other hand, little had been revealed as to the value that would accrue from His resurrection. That particular event, being more related to the New Creation than to the old, was, to some extent, withheld as a part of the "mystery."

The Mystery Revealed

What then is the "mystery?" It is stated in verse 6 in the simplest of terms: "That the Gentiles should be fellow-heirs, and of the same body, and partakers of his promise in Christ by the gospel." This declaration must not be treated lightly. That the Gentiles should be fellow heirs and of the same body is not a recognition of the Old Testament prediction that, during Israel's coming kingdom glory, Gentiles will be raised to a subordinate participation in those blessings (Isa. 60:12). Those predictions were of an earthly calling, and, being revealed in very much Old Testament prophecy, could be no part of the heavenly calling—the "mystery hid in God." This mystery is of a present uniting of Jews and Gentiles into one body—a new divine purpose, and, therefore, in no sense the perpetuation of anything which has been before.

Wonderful and startling indeed is the fact that heavenly blessings are now accorded to Gentiles. It will be remembered that they were without promise (2:12); but now they have promise *in Christ* by the Gospel. Just as wonderful and equally as startling is the assertion that Jews are to partake with Gentiles in this "one body." This divine offer of a possible entrance into the New Creation is no part of Israel's hope. So far as this new divine purpose is concerned, Israel was as much "without hope" as the Gentiles. At that time no disposition existed on the part of the Jew to be united into one body with the Gentile, nor is he naturally so disposed today. No more drastic innovation in the divine dealing with men had ever been announced than was announced by the Apostle Paul at the beginning of this age—that, as to Gospel privilege and the entrance into the New Creation in Christ Jesus, there is no difference between Jew and Gentile (Rom. 3:9; 10:12). The national covenants which belong to Israel are never said to be realized in the present dispensation of the Church. They are, rather, as originally predicted, to be fulfilled in the coming Messianic Kingdom. On the other hand, the Gospel, which is now proclaimed by the authority of God and in the power of the Spirit, offers the Kingdom to no one—neither Jew nor Gentile.

That the Church is a new purpose of God could not be more clearly stated than it is in verses 3 to 9, yet certain schools of theology contend that the Church in her present form is but a continuation of God's one purpose from the beginning of the human family. They speak of an "Old Testament church" and seek to relate this to the one body which constitutes the New Testament revelation. The fact that Jews are now invited into fellowheirship in one body with Gentiles is no warrant for the belief that Old Testament saints are included in this new divine purpose. Arguments for an Old Testament church are usually based on: (1) the fact that the Old Testament sacrifices looked forward to Christ; (2) that Israel was a sanctified nation; (3) that there was a godly remnant in each of Israel's generations; (4) that the Septuagint translates the word which indicates an assembly or gathering of people by the word *ekklesia;* and (5) since all saints go to heaven, they must, because of that fact, constitute one company.

These arguments are insufficient at every point. (1) The sacrifice of Christ serves for both dispensations and looks backward as well as forward (Rom. 3:25, 26). (2) There are multiplied distinctions to be drawn between Israel and the Church whereby they are seen to be different in almost every particular. (3) The remnant were none other than members of the nation with no special privilege. They did, however, cleave closer to God as individuals and thus realized more of the divine blessings. (4) The word *ekklesia* is properly used of a gathering of people at any time and anywhere, but this does not constitute any congregation in Israel to be the body and bride of Christ. (5) There will be many gathered together in the heavenly city, but not all will be on the same plane of privilege, nor will they be designated alike. In Hebrews 12:22-24, where the inhabitants of the heavenly city are enumerated, we read of the "spirits of just men made perfect" and also of the "church of the first-born." These could not possibly be one and the same company. Likewise, there are mansions which will be occupied in heaven (John 14:1-3), but not by the Church; for Christ said, "I go to prepare a place for you."

Questions That Need an Answer

The assertion that the New Testament *mystery in Christ* is composed of all saints in all the ages seems to lack a consideration of the issues involved. If the Church is a continuous purpose of God throughout the dispensations, why the rent veil? Why Pentecost? Why the distinctive message of the Epistles which is properly identified as *Church truth?* Why the "better things" of the book of Hebrews? Why were Jewish branches broken off? Why the present headship and ministry of Christ in heaven? Why the visitation of the Gentiles *now* and not before? Why the present indwelling by the Spirit of *all who believe?* Why the baptism of the Spirit, unique in the New Testament? Why two companies of redeemed in heaven? Why only earthly promises to Israel, and only heavenly promises to the Church?

Why did Christ confine His early ministry to Israel and yet in the end of that ministry direct His disciples to go into all the world? Why should the divinely given rule of life be changed from law to grace? Why is Israel likened to the *repudiated wife* of Jehovah, and the Church likened to the *espoused bride* of Christ? Why the new day—the *Day of Christ*—with its rapture and resurrection of believers, with its rewards for service and suffering—a day never seen in the Old Testament? Why the mysteries in the New Testament, including that new body *in Christ*? And why the New Creation comprising, as it does, all those who by the Spirit are joined to the Lord and so *forever in Christ*? How could there be a Church, constructed as she is, until the death of Christ, the resurrection of Christ, the ascension of Christ, and the Day of Pentecost? How could the Church, in which there is neither Jew nor Gentile, be any part of Israel in this or any other age?

If these questions, and the many more that might be propounded, are answered from the Scriptures, the conclusion must be that the Church, the New Creation in Christ, which is made up of both Jew and Gentile, is a new purpose of God and constitutes the primary divine objective of this age.

In verses 7, 8, and 9, the Apostle contends for his unique position as the one chosen of God for the reception and declaration of the new message concerning the *mystery in Christ*. In verse 10 he declares that it is through the Church that the angelic hosts *now* know the *manifold wisdom of God*; as, in 2:7, the angels are, in the ages to come, to know by the Church the *exceeding riches of the grace of God*. All of this disclosure concerning the Church and her present ministry to the principalities and powers as a revelation of God's wisdom is, likewise (*cf.* 1:9), according to the eternal purpose which He purposed in Christ Jesus our Lord (verse 11).

It is given to the angelic hosts to observe that, through our faith in Christ, we have boldness, free intimacy with God, and introduction into His blessed fellowship; but how great is the privilege granted to those who experience this intimacy and fellowship!

This parenthetical passage which discloses the marvels of the new divine purpose in the Church, which offers the highest celestial glory to both Jew and Gentile alike, closes with expressed solicitude of the Apostle (verse 12) lest these Ephesian believers faint because of his tribulation for them. He is convinced that, because of the glory which is theirs *in Christ*, his own sufferings for them are abundantly worth while.

Section Ten

Ephesians 3:14-21

14 For this cause I bow my knees unto the Father of our Lord
Jesus Christ,

15 Of whom the whole family in heaven and earth is named,

16 That he would grant you, according to the riches of his glory,
to be strengthened with might by his Spirit in the inner man;

17 That Christ may dwell in your hearts by faith; that ye, being
rooted and grounded in love,

18 May be able to comprehend with all saints what is the breadth,
and length, and depth, and height;

19 And to know the love of Christ, which passeth knowledge,
that ye might be filled with all the fulness of God.

20 Now unto him that is able to do exceeding abundantly above
all that we ask or think, according to the power that worketh
in us,

21 Unto him be glory in the church by Christ Jesus throughout all
ages, world without end. Amen.

The parenthetical portion (3:1-13) being concluded, the
Apostle resumes (3:14) the theme with which Chapter two
closed. The thought of the Church in its corporate whole as a
growing building of living stones in which God by His Spirit is
pleased to dwell, now shifts to the experience of each individual who, being saved, has a share in that eternal structure. Here
the Apostle recites those habitual desires of his heart toward
God which enter into his oft-repeated prayers in behalf of the
Ephesian believers. In this there is a close similarity to the former
passage (1:15-23) where, as before pointed out, the Apostle is
not then offering a prayer, but is rather indicating those themes

which, being the constant burden of his heart, find expression in all his prayers. The first recital of prayer subjects includes his desire that the Spirit of wisdom and revelation may be given unto them that they may know from the heart what is the hope of His calling, and what are the riches of the glory of His inheritance in the saints; so, also, the exceeding greatness of His power to all who believe. Whereas, in this second recital of his prayer themes he indicates that he prays that they may be able to comprehend, not now the marvels of their own position in Christ, but the marvels of the knowledge-surpassing love of Christ; to this end being strengthened in the inner man by the same Spirit.

A Sacred Secret

However, in the preceding notable parenthesis much has been added to the sum-total of the revelation concerning the Church. While it is disclosed in Chapter two that a perfect union has been secured between those of Israel and those of the Gentiles who believe, this union constitutes one body of which Christ is the Head, and one building of which He is the Chief Corner Stone. It is revealed in the parenthetical passage that the forming of this one body from these widely separated peoples is a sacred secret hid in ages past and is therefore not a continuation of any former divine purpose. The Church in which the saved from among the Jews and from among the Gentiles are united is one eternal, heavenly fellowship and glory, and is the realization of a celestial, divine purpose far surpassing anything that ever was or ever will be on the earth. If the Church now serves to manifest the "manifold wisdom of God" before principalities and powers (3:10), so she will, in the ages to come, display the "exceeding riches of his grace" (2:7).

No such purpose characterized the divine undertaking as set forth in the Old Testament and, aside from the hope of heaven accorded to the individual saint who was renewed by the Spirit of God, there is in view in the Old Testament only an earthly destiny for an earthly people. They are to be regathered to their own land and there experience a marvelous glory, but it is a glory of the earth and not of heaven. No wider distinction could be created in the destinies of men than exists between

Israel the nation, centered forever, as she is, in the earth, and the Church, belonging, as she does, only to heaven. If these two divine purposes are confused, there can be little understanding of the distinctive truth which the first section of this Epistle reveals, nor is there any adequate basis of the appeal which follows for a heavenly walk.

Much is contemplated by the first phrase of Chapter three, which phrase is again repeated as the parenthesis closes and at the beginning of verse 14, "For this cause"; that is, because of the limitless privilege accorded these believers in that they have been saved from the lost estate (2:13) to the heavenly glory (2:4 to 3:13), the Apostle bows his knees to the Father of our Lord Jesus Christ of Whom all the family in heaven and earth is named. The object of the prayer which he here recounts is threefold.

A New Way to Pray

However, before entering into the features of his prayer, attention should be given to the important word with which the record of the prayer is introduced.

The Apostle declares that he bows his knees to the Father of our Lord Jesus Christ. Aside from the posture of prayer which is here indicated, the fact that the prayer is addressed to the *Father* is of great importance conforming, as it does, with the specific teachings of Christ. Anticipating the present age with the heavenly relationships and privileges which are now accorded to the members of His body He said, "And in that day ye shall ask me nothing. Verily, verily, I say unto you, Whatsoever ye shall ask the Father in my name, he will give it you" (John 16:23). Christ thus reveals the new ground of prayer, namely, that it is now to be addressed to the Father in the name and mediation of the Son. Thus a perfect access to God is secured and a freedom is gained whereby the Father may not only hear us as He hears the Son, but may grant to us His limitless bounty as He would grant it to His Son.

Prayer which is addressed to Christ not only ignores His direct teaching that we are not now to ask Him anything, but becomes prayer *to* the Mediator rather than *through* the Mediator. Surely this is no slight error, and the Apostle is careful to record that he addresses his prayer to the *Father*, Who is indeed the Father of our Lord Jesus Christ—a filial relationship which could have no **beginning**, nor can it have an ending. The Father is also here declared to be the One of Whom the whole family in heaven and earth is named. The phrase *"the whole family"* being better rendered *"every fatherhood"*—naturally meaning those families wherein He is Father. The breadth of this relationship on the earth, let alone the vast unexplored associations in heaven, cannot be measured. Withal, His Fatherhood is personal and real in the case of the least of all saints, and will continue to be throughout the ages of the ages.

In the opening portion of this Epistle, the sovereignty of God has been emphasized. It has there been revealed that all things work according to the counsel of His will. If this truth stood alone there would be little to be gained by prayer, but it does not stand alone; there is a human as well as a divine side to the progress and life of each individual, and like every union of the divine and human—as in the Person of our adorable Lord, and in the Scriptures of Truth—the divine is not disqualified by its union with the human, nor is the human exalted by its union with the divine. In the field of prayer, it is clear, on the one hand, that there is that aspect of it in which God's unalterable purpose is to be realized with the absoluteness of Infinity. To this end, the Spirit, Who knows the mind of God, prays through the believer according to the *will* of God (Rom. 8:26, 27); and effectual prayer, it is disclosed, must be in the name of the Son, that the Father may be glorified in the Son (John 14:13).

Conversely, it is equally true that, on the human side, men are enjoined to *ask, to seek* and *to knock*; the implication being that "prayer changes things." The Apostle knows full well that the divine purpose in behalf of the Ephesian saints will be executed to perfection, but he also knows that it is a part of that divine purpose that he shall cooperate through the ministry of prayer, and that, from the human side, it is most imperative that he bow his knees and request God to grant these foreordained blessings to those for whom he prays.

How much of theological controversy might have been avoided and how much more of divine blessing might have been secured in past days had men been willing to allow both the divine and human aspects of truth to continue side by side unimpaired! Rather, men have too often insisted that, if the purpose of God is foreordained, there can be no room for the human responsibility. Likewise, others have as urgently insisted that, if there is a human responsibility, there is no unchangeable sovereignty in the will of God.

There could be no doubt but that the Apostle Paul believed in the divine sovereignty, yet he prayed that God would grant three important blessings to these saints, and he prayed with evident confidence that *prayer does change things*.

First, "That he would grant you, according to the riches of his glory, to be strengthened with might by his Spirit in the inner man." Thus the Apostle prays that the Holy Spirit may strengthen the inner life of these saints according to the sublime measurement of the riches of divine glory. This is the first mention of that theme—the life that is energized by the Holy Spirit— which is yet to occupy so large a place in this Epistle.

Too Marvelous for the Mind

To be strengthened with might by His Spirit in the inner man, and upon the plane of the riches of God's infinite glory, is a request concerning things too marvelous for the human mind to grasp. Such divine energizing may be unto the exercise of a gift, unto effectual intercession, unto a holy walk, unto celestial joy, or unto a quickened spiritual understanding; but the spiritual understanding is most evidently in view here. During a period of more than three years the disciples were privileged to sit at Christ's feet and to learn of Him. He taught them most effectively, but within certain limitations; for at the end of this season He said to them, "I have yet many things to say unto you, but ye cannot bear them now. Howbeit when he, the Spirit of truth, is come, he will guide you into all truth: for he shall not speak of himself; but whatsoever he shall hear, that shall he speak: and he will shew you things to come. He shall glorify me: for he shall receive of mine, and shall shew it unto you. All things that the Father hath are mine: therefore said I, that he shall take of mine, and shall shew it unto you" (John 16:12-15).

The strong indication is that, until the Spirit came and took up His abode in them, certain truths could not be comprehended. Thus, even the divine instructions are, because of human limitations, classified in two general widely differing divisions—that which the unaided mind might grasp, and that which cannot be revealed apart from the immediate and personal ministry of the Holy Spirit in taking of the things of Christ and showing them unto us. Hence, it will be observed that the objective in view in this petition was not for divine enablement unto outward activity and service, but rather that the believer might be enabled in general to enjoy the blessed portion which is his *in Christ* (this portion having been described at length in the first chapter of this Epistle), and that he may be enabled in particular to know the knowledge-surpassing love of Christ, and so be filled with all the fulness of God. Of all the spheres in which the Spirit energizes the believer, there is none comparable to this that the inner man should be strengthened to know the love of the Lord Jesus Christ, and to be thus strengthened according to "the riches of his glory." Could there be a greater sin on the part of the believer than that, when such heavenly association on the plane of heavenly glory is provided, he should continue to dwell on the lower level of the carnal man?

The Indwelling Christ

The second prayer petition which the Apostle here recounts is "that Christ may dwell in your hearts by faith." There is a logical sequence here. The thing desired in this second petition is the sure result of the realization of the first petition; for when the inner man is strengthened by the Spirit, it is accompanied by the flooding of the heart with a greater realization of the Person and Presence of Christ. It is the Spirit's ministry to disclose not Himself but Christ (John 16:12-15). By a careful reading of Chapters thirteen to seventeen of John's Gospel, the almost limitless field of supernatural knowledge concerning Christ which the Spirit will impart is revealed.

It is pertinent to inquire at this point as to the precise meaning of the petition "that Christ may *dwell* in your hearts by faith." True, the tense of this verb indicates that this is not a mere continuous dwelling, but is rather His coming to dwell as a single, definite act. Does the Apostle imply that all Ephesian believers were, until this time, void of the indwelling Christ? Such a meaning would be impossible. There are two most vital facts which distinguish the Christian as such—he is *in Christ* as to position, and Christ is *in Him* as to the possession of the divine nature. Indeed, the Apostle has written, "Now if any man have not the Spirit of Christ, he is none of his" (Rom. 8:9), and again, "Know ye not your own selves, how that Jesus Christ is in you, except ye be reprobates?" (2 Cor. 13:5). From what has gone before in this Epistle (2:1, 5, 6, 13), there can be no question as to the genuineness of the salvation of those to whom he is writing. Therefore, there can be no question as to the fact that Christ was then indwelling each and every one of them. The Apostle is not here making petition that these believers may be indwelt, but rather that they may come by faith into a fuller knowledge of the indwelling Christ. To this end he desires for them that Christ may ever be coming more into their con-sciousness as the One Who is nearer to each of them than the members of their own bodies.

Filled with All Fulness

The third petition is the completion of this sequence. It is, "that ye, being rooted and grounded in love, may be able to comprehend with all saints what is the breadth, and length, and depth, and height; and to know the love of Christ, which passeth knowledge, that ye might be filled with all the fulness of God" (verses 17-19). The love in which they might be rooted and grounded is not some feeble love these believers might experience toward God, but it is the love of God toward them— the love which has chosen them, which has predestined them, which has adopted them, which has made them accepted in the Beloved, which has redeemed them, which has provided an inheritance for them, which has sealed them by the Spirit, which has quickened them, and which has raised them and seated them in the heavenly in Christ Jesus. To be rooted and grounded in such love is to have entered sympathetically and understandingly into the measureless revelation of that love. So, also, with this experience of understanding of the divine love in general, there is to be a comprehending of the knowl-edge-surpassing love of Christ in particular. Graphic, indeed, is the language employed here which assigns to this particular love the dimensions of space—"breadth," "length," "depth," and "height—but these are dimensions which are infinite.

This marvelous understanding and comprehending by a Spirit-strengthened inner man, and upon the plane of celestial glory, can result in nothing less than that those thus enriched will be "filled with *all* the fulness of God." The fact that they will be "filled with all the fulness of God" needs careful consideration. Only one among all that ever dwelt on earth or in heaven has been really filled with all the fulness of God. In Colossians 2:9, 10, we read of Christ that "in him dwelleth all the fulness of the Godhead bodily," and that the believer is "complete in him." So, again, in John 1:16 it is declared that "of his fulness have all we received, and grace for grace." God alone is the Container of all things, and not man. Likewise, all fullness dwells in Christ, but not in us. We may be filled with the fulness (Greek, *pleeroma*—a great New Testament word—*cf.* Eph. 1:10, 23; 3:19; and 4:13) of God in that sense which is presented in the context. We may come by the Spirit's strengthening to comprehend the knowledge of Him (1:17; Col. 1:10), of His will (Col. 1:9), of His glory (2 Cor. 4:6), and of His love (Eph. 3:19); and what God is to us as the Father of our Lord Jesus Christ we shall be learning throughout eternity.

Both the record of these prayer petitions and the entire first section of this Epistle are closed by one and the same doxology (3:20, 21), which doxology is eminently fitting. All the glory is to be ascribed to God Who is the Father of the Savior and of the saints. He it is to Whom the Son ascribes all glory forever (John 13:31; 14:13), and unto His glory and according to His perfect will He is working all things in behalf of those whom He has chosen and redeemed (1:11, 12). His eternal purposes, both in the Church and in Christ Jesus, are *superlative* even in the realms of infinity and heaven. Yet He is *able* to do all that He has purposed, which is here said to be more, indeed, than we can ask or think (understand); yea, and *"exceeding abundantly"* above this measure. What He purposed is none other than all that has been revealed in the early portion of this Epistle. Every spiritual blessing *in Christ* is in view, and these the Apostle has by the Spirit set forth in Chapters one to three. This surpassing glory, which is to be to the Father through the Church—for she is chosen in Him before the foundation of the world to the praise of His glory—and in the Son Who ascribes all glory to the Father, is a glory that endures "throughout all ages, world without end. Amen."

Section Eleven
Ephesians 4:1-6

1 I therefore, the prisoner of the Lord, beseech you that ye walk worthy of the vocation wherewith ye are called,

2 With all lowliness and meekness, with longsuffering, forbearing one another in love;

3 Endeavoring to keep the unity of the Spirit in the bond of peace.

4 There is one body, and one Spirit, even as ye are called in one hope of your calling;

5 One Lord, one faith, one baptism,

6 One God and Father of all, who is above all, and through all, and in you all.

This Epistle, like other doctrinal letters of the New Testament, divides into two main divisions. Of the six chapters which represent the entire context, the first division is completed in the first three chapters, and the second division is completed in the last three chapters. These two divisions bear a vital relation to each other. Perhaps no better indication of this fact will be found than that the second section, which begins with 4:1, is introduced by the words "I therefore." It is thereby indicated that the preceding portion, setting forth the riches of divine grace (Chapters 1-3), is now followed by its sequel in which is set forth that manner of life and conduct which becomes those who are thus enriched in the measureless divine grace. According to the divine purpose, doctrine often finds its expression in a life that is consistent and compatible with the exalted position and privilege which the doctrine connotes. It is easily recognized that the son of a king should so act as to grace his royal position, and, too, it is as easily recognized that this order could not be reversed to the extent that one might become the son of a king by the mere assumption of royal conduct.

The relative importance of the exalted position as compared with the consistent life which it imposes is obvious. One is unto a vital and eternal transformation of being, while the other is an ethical and momentary problem of conduct—an obligation growing normally out of the more or less incidental fact that the saved one continues to live here on the earth after the divine transformation is wrought. It would be simple indeed, and in no way diminishing of the divine transformation, should the Christian at the moment he is saved, like the dying thief, be immediately called away from this world into scenes of glory and thus be deprived of even a moment of Christian life and responsibility on the earth.

Incomparable, indeed, at every point are the two issues which are presented in the two main divisions of this Epistle. One represents what God in sovereign grace can do for man; the other represents what man in a life of devotion and service may do for God. One accomplishes the marvels of the infinite and eternal purpose of God; the other but feebly acknowledges this benefit by a life which is characterized by its brevity and which to some degree seeks to be consistent to that benefit. Since the divine benefit is no less than the fact that the saved one is raised and seated in the heavenly in Christ Jesus, the corresponding manner of life is no less than that which would normally be required of any heavenly citizen.

A Contrast in Principles

At every point of comparison there is sharp contrast to be noted in these heavenly principles of grace and those earthly principles which governed Israel in the land in the age gone by. Israel's blessing—always earthly—depended upon her faithful conduct; the formula of the law is, "Be good and I will bless you"; while for the Church, the divine blessing in saving grace is wrought to an infinite degree before any human merit can be introduced, and the grace relationship is indicated by the formula, "I have blessed you; now be good." In like manner, the legal demands addressed to Israel, though as holy and pure as the God Who gave them, were, in the main, such as might be wrought by unaided man; while the demands under grace are such as can be wrought only by the supernatural power which comes through the energy of the indwelling Spirit. Such considerations as these, added to what has gone before, may well serve to emphasize again the fact that the Church is not identical with Israel.

Before entering into the practical appeal, which is the message of the second division of this Epistle, it may be advantageous to review briefly the message of the first division that the order of this sublime truth may again be observed and the force of its appeal may be strengthened.

A New Creation

Four books in the Bible are characterized by the fact that they each in their opening portions set forth the beginnings of some great work or purpose of God. Genesis records the beginning of the creation of material things, life upon the earth, and all things belonging to the old and ruined order. The Gospel of John records the Logos from all eternity and the beginning of His ever-abiding Theanthropic Person. The Book of Hebrews records the beginning of God's written Word spoken first through the prophets and afterwards through His Son. The Epistle to the Ephesians records the beginning of the New Creation—the Church and her relation to Christ.

True to the plan and method of sovereign grace, the opening theme of the Ephesian letter, descriptive of the Church, is that before any individual who belongs to her company has wrought anything for God, that individual is graciously blessed with every spiritual blessing in the heavenly in Christ. He is chosen in Him before the foundation of the world, destined to His eternal glory, and to this end is redeemed through the blood of Christ. This redemption has been from the lowest estate of the lost to the most exalted position in heavenly glory, and each individual who shares in the heavenly company is appointed to manifest the wisdom of God now, and "in the ages to come" to manifest the grace of God to all principalities and powers. Drawn from both Jews and Gentiles, each and everyone of those who share in His body is saved unto the ultimate perfection and likeness of Christ, and is energized by the indwelling Spirit. The individual believer is now a child of God, a citizen of heaven, of the family and household of God, and destined to share forever in the heavenly glory with Christ. Such is the testimony of the first division of this Epistle.

How ought such an one to walk here on the earth during the moments of time which intervene between his salvation and his final translation into celestial glory? Certainly his motive for right conduct is not now on a legal basis which would be that, by good conduct, he may obtain these riches of grace. The riches, being riches of *grace*, are divinely conferred on the one who believes and before human conduct is considered. Therefore, the only appeal now is for a walk which is worthy of a calling wherewith the saved one is called. How simple and how sublime and how efficacious is this motive for God-honoring conduct! The believer does not strive to attain a position, but rather to live well-pleasing unto God in the position already attained through divine grace. Thus it is seen that grace not only saves one who trusts in Christ, but that grace automatically sets up a new obligation of a consistent walk and service according to a high standard surpassing any standard ever known before. It is the believer's life under grace. Of this life and service the second division of this Epistle treats.

Having set forth the revelation of the believer's heavenly position as declared in the first division of the Epistle, the Apostle now turns to the practical appeal which is based upon that revelation. He states, "I, therefore, the prisoner of the Lord [in the Lord] beseech you that you walk worthy of the vocation [calling] wherewith ye are called." In the phrase, *the calling wherewith ye are called*, two forms of the same word appear. In each instance the calling to which reference is made is no less than the heavenly position into which the believer has been brought through infinite grace, which position naturally prescribes a corresponding holy manner of life. Thus the message of the first division of the book is not now left behind, but is carried on as the impelling principle which motivates every spiritual action. In verses 2 and 3, five distinct virtues are indicated which, in turn, should characterize a life which is so signally exalted and blessed in Christ Jesus. These virtues are:

Lowliness

As a virtue, lowliness stands first in this list. Indeed, it would be natural for the flesh to be lifted up with pride because of the exalted position obtained. However, to correct effectively such pride it need only be remembered that the exaltation is altogether the workmanship of God through grace, and not of works lest any man should boast. Lowliness, which is an unaffected lowly estimate of self, is reasonable, and because of the fact that to Him alone belongs all the glory forever. Even Christ in the sphere of His humanity was "meek and lowly in heart" (Matt. 11:29); and, upon the human side in His own dependence upon His Father, Christ is the pattern of all true creature-dependence. How much more, then, does lowliness belong to those whom He has redeemed from the lowest estate of the lost! Being dependent upon God for every good, there is no basis for glory in any other than in the One from Whom all blessings flow. It is most significant that the Apostle should name *lowliness* first as being a true heart-adjustment to an outward manifestation of the heavenly calling.

Meekness

This word implies patience in trial and persecution; and by so much the believer is momentarily drawn from the contemplation of his high calling to the recognition of the fact that the world is at enmity with God and therefore is at enmity with His redeemed ones. Christ said, "If the world hate you, ye know that it hated me before it hated you" (John 15:18). Thus, having first noted that virtue which is the manifestation of a true recognition of the new relation to God in grace, the Apostle then presents *meekness* as the manifestation of a true recognition of the believer's new relation to the world. Of all virtues, meekness lends itself less than any other to imitation. It utterly lacks substance or reality when disassociated from the state of mind and heart which recognizes that all one's springs are in Him (Ps. 87:7).

Longsuffering

The third virtue in this list is one closely related elsewhere with meekness (*cf.* Gal. 5:22; Col. 3:12), and is likewise a divine characteristic (Rom. 2:4; 9:22; 1 Tim. 1:16; 1 Pet. 3:20; 2 Pet. 3:15). Longsuffering may be drawn out because of relationship to other believers, or because of relationship to the unregenerate. In each and every case, it becomes the child of God who is redeemed, and who is appointed while in this world to show forth the virtues of Him Who called him out of darkness into His marvelous light (1 Pet. 2:9). It is divine love which "suffers long and is kind," and this virtue belongs to those who are *in Him*.

Forbearing one another in love

Forbearance is needed, as is longsuffering, since the children of God are yet in this world and subject to the great limitations that now characterize humanity; limitations, it is true, that may be overcome by the indwelling Spirit, but which, alas, are too often not overcome and therefore are the occasion of forbearance and longsuffering on the part of those who associate with them. The exhortation is not concerning relationship to those outside the household and family of God, but it has in view the fellowship with the saints. The forbearance of God, like His longsuffering, is ever manifest, and these virtues are essential in the lives of those who are His own. Let it be repeated, there surely will be occasion for such forbearance. In the Colossian letter we read: "Forbearing one another, and forgiving one another, if any man have a quarrel against any: even as Christ forgave you, so also do ye" (Col. 3:13). This is true Christlikeness and belongs entirely to those who are "in Him."

Endeavoring [diligently striving] to keep the unity of the Spirit in the bond of peace

The unity of the Spirit which the saints are here enjoined to *"keep"* is that oneness which has been consummated by the Spirit Who has already united them to Christ in one body thereby making peace (2:15). Nowhere are the children of God appointed to the impossible task of *making* a union, though this task is too often undertaken in good will by those who have not learned to recognize the sacred bond within the one body, which bond has been secured by Christ.

Ours is rather to keep the unity which Christ has made, and

in the bond of peace which that unity provides. Practically, this responsibility is intensely individual; it is simply that each Christian is expected to recognize and love every other Christian. Who can doubt the reality of this experience as described in the record of the early Church (Acts 2:44-46; 4:32-37)? So sacred indeed were these bonds of practical unity that Ananias and Sapphira were stricken with instant death because of a mere pretense of a whole-hearted devotion to the Christian community. In the complexity of modern life and the multitude of those who profess the Name of Christ, there are problems arising which did not then exist. Nowhere in the Bible account do we find so many believers in one locality that there needed to be two assemblies in that locality with the attending possibilities of rivalry and sectarian division; and there is no excuse for sectarian strife today. Let each child of God discharge his own responsibility to the end that he love every other child of God with a pure heart fervently. The result so much to be desired will be, not the *making* of unity nor the *making* of peace; but rather the *keeping* of that unity which already exists in the one body, with its attending peace. Such devotion is the never-failing insignia of divine relationship: "By this shall men know that ye are my disciples, if ye have love one to another" (John 13:35). This is no mere human love; it is rather an imparted divine love which is measured as to its degree by the words, *"As I have loved you"* (John 13:34; 15:12, 17).

All that the Apostle beseeches—"walk worthy," "lowliness," "meekness," "longsuffering," "forbearance," and keeping of the unity—are superhuman traits and anticipate that the believer will give diligence to secure these by the God-provided means through the indwelling Spirit.

Beginning with verse 4, the Apostle enumerates the features which are the very ground of that unity and peace to which reference has been made. Seven of these are mentioned, and they are basal characteristics of the new relation between the Triune God and His heavenly, blood-bought people—the Church.

There is "one body"

The imagery here, as throughout the New Testament, is of a

human body with its head and its many members. The Ephesian letter presents the most extensive development of this conception of the Church (1:23; 2:15, 16; 3:6; 4:12-14; 5:30). If the human body is a means of manifestation of the invisible human life, so the Church is the manifestation of Christ to the world.

Likewise, as the many members are privileged to serve, each in its appointed sphere in the human body, so each individual believer serves the living Head. However, the specific truth in view at this point is that of *unity;* and of this aspect of relationship between Christ and the Church and between the members themselves, there could be no more vivid portrayal than is set forth by the figure of the human body. Here, as in the following verities, the word *one* is emphatic, signifying that there is but *one* body—not two, and certainly not three hundred to correspond to the present number of sects in Christendom. Every saved person is in this unity, and only those who are saved are included in it.

There is "one Spirit"

The Third Person of the Trinity is in view. He Who convicts (John 16:7-11), Who regenerates (John 3:5, 6), Who indwells (1 Cor. 6:19), Who seals (Eph. 1:13), Who baptizes (1 Cor. 12:13), Who fills (Eph. 5:18), and, whether there be many gifts, there is but "one Spirit" (1 Cor. 12:4). Thus it is revealed that the ministries He performs are all *unifying* to the utmost degree.

There is "one hope of your calling"

The *hope* belongs to the new sphere unto which the saints are called (1:18). It embraces all that God has promised of that eternal glory which is to be consummated at the coming of Christ. Here, as usual in the New Testament, the Christian hope is centered in that great event and, as the hope is one as to its provision for each and every believer alike, it becomes itself a *unifying* hope.

There is "one Lord"

Doubtless the Second Person of the Trinity is here contemplated and as to His *Lordship.* As Head over all things to the Church, He is now not only their Authority and Possessor, but He *unifies* them into one heavenly people.

There is "one faith"

Not now that uniform need of faith unto salvation or service which must characterize all saints is in view, but the thought is, that there is *one* body of truth committed to them and only *one*, which body of truth is designated as *the faith* (*cf.* Luke 18:8; Jude 3). This body of truth, incorporating as it does the distinctive New Testament revelation, is another *unifying* agency of measureless effectiveness.

There is "one baptism"

Not two; though the New Testament distinguishes the real baptism with the Spirit from the *ritual* baptism with water; and since, according to this passage, there is but *one* baptism, it is needless to inquire as to which baptism is in view. In explaining this emphasis upon the one baptism, some claim that *real* baptism is so much more important than *ritual* baptism that *ritual* baptism could not be mentioned with propriety in the midst of these heaven-high verities in which the *one* baptism appears. Others point out that the two baptisms, like substance and shadow, are so closely related to each other as to form *one* baptism, and thus both are *included* in the one. On the one hand, to those who believe that *ritual* baptism is in itself an individual, diverse, and unrelated procedure, having no relation to the baptizing work of the Spirit, this latter view will not be agreeable; and for these, in spite of the statement that there is but one, the question continues unanswered as to which baptism is indicated in this passage. To those who believe that *ritual* baptism is but the outward sign or symbol of *real* baptism, there is no difficulty created by this emphasis upon *one* baptism.

Apparently no one ministry of the Spirit accomplishes so much for the believer as does His baptism, by which we are joined to the Lord, and, being thus *in Him*, we are made partakers of all that He is, even every spiritual blessing in Christ Jesus. Certainly this all-important real baptism is not here set aside as unworthy of consideration and as secondary to *ritual* baptism; nor could it be said of any form of *ritual* baptism that it is a unifying agency. The history of the Church is a counterwitness to this. However, the *real* baptism which joins all believers to Christ is certainly a *unifying* agency beyond measure.

There is "one God and Father"

This, the last of these verities, completes the recognition of the blessed Trinity, and that the unifying effect of *one* Father's relation to the Church may be apprehended, it is distinctly declared that He is "above all," "through all," and "in you all."

The Apostle thus presents the strongest possible appeal for Christian unity, indicating as he does that it is grounded upon these seven eternal verities. It therefore becomes those who by grace have attained to heavenly positions to manifest that fact by unfeigned love to all who are in Christ.

Section Twelve

Ephesians 4:7-16

7 But unto every one of us is given grace according to the measure of the gift of Christ.

8 Wherefore he saith, When he ascended up on high, he led captivity captive, and gave gifts unto men.

9 (Now that he ascended, what is it but that he also descended first into the lower parts of the earth?

10 He that descended is the same also that ascended up far above all heavens, that he might fill all things.)

11 And he gave some, apostles; and some, prophets; and some, evangelists; and some, pastors and teachers;

12 For the perfecting of the saints, for the work of the ministry, for the edifying of the body of Christ:

13 Till we all come in the unity of the faith, and of the knowledge of the Son of God, unto a perfect man, unto the measure of the stature of the fulness of Christ:

14 That we henceforth be no more children, tossed to and fro, and carried about with every wind of doctrine, by the sleight of men, and cunning craftiness whereby they lie in wait to deceive;

15 But speaking the truth in love, may grow up into him in all things, which is the head, even Christ:

16 From whom the whole body fitly joined together and compacted by that which every joint supplieth, according to the effectual working in the measure of every part, maketh increase of the body unto the edifying of itself in love.

The preceding portion of this Chapter has given particular emphasis to those great fundamental facts of the Christian faith which are at once its unifying features. The Apostle now turns to the consideration of that diversity of gifts which characterizes the fellowship of the saints in the prosecution of the ministry committed unto them; which ministry is, by divine intent, unto the building up and completion of the Church —the body of Christ. The unity is not forgotten; it is rather that which binds together in one incomparable organism all those who, under God, may serve in the exercise of diversified gifts.

By the words, "But unto every one of us is given grace according to the measure of the gift of Christ" (verse 7), the important New Testament doctrine of the Holy Spirit's divine enablement in service is introduced. The Holy Spirit of God Who, as seen in 3:16, is the One Who strengthens with might in the inner man, and in 4:3 as one of the potent unifying agencies of the Body of Christ, is the Administrator of those varying gifts which are bestowed by the exalted Son of God. That the Spirit administers and gives strength for the exercise of the gifts is declared in other portions of Scripture.

In Romans 12:3-8 we read, "For I say, through the grace given unto me, to every man that is among you, not to think of himself more highly than he ought to think; but to think soberly, according as God hath dealt to every man the measure of faith. For as we have many members in one body, and all members have not the same office: so we, being many, are one body in Christ, and every one members one of another. Having then gifts differing according to the grace that is given to us, whether prophecy, let us prophesy according to the proportion of faith; or ministry, let us wait on our ministering; or he that teacheth, on teaching; or he that exhorteth, on exhortation: he that giveth, let him do it with simplicity; he that ruleth, with diligence; he that sheweth mercy, with cheerfulness"; and again in 1 Corinthians 12:4-11, "Now there are diversities of gifts, but the same Spirit. And there are differences of administrations, but the same Lord, and there are diversities of operations, but it is the same God which worketh all in all. But the manifestation of the Spirit is given to every man to profit withal. For to one is given by the Spirit the word of wisdom; to another the word of knowledge by the same Spirit; to another faith by the same Spirit; to another the gifts of healing by the same Spirit; to another the working of miracles; to another prophecy; to another discerning of spirits; to another divers kinds of tongues; and to another the interpretation of tongues; but all these worketh that one and the selfsame Spirit, dividing to every man severally as he will"; so, also, 1 Peter 4:10-11, "As every man hath received the gift, even so minister the same one to another, as good stewards of the manifold grace of God. If any man speak, let him speak as the oracles of God; if any man minister, let him do it as of the ability which God giveth: that God in all things may be glorified through Jesus Christ, to whom be praise and dominion for ever and ever. Amen."

The Diversity of Gifts

Thus all true God-appointed service is seen to be the exercise by the Spirit of the gift of Christ, and the emphasis in all this Scripture is on the *diversity* of the gifts. In fact, since no two of God's children are situated in identically the same circumstances nor called of Him to identically the same service, there are no two who are precisely alike in their divine appointments. Thus each and every believer confronts the solemn, individual responsibility of completing the task which is to be undertaken by none other than himself, and which he may believe represents a thought of God which is nowhere else to be represented in the world.

In the New Testament use of the word, a *gift* is quite removed from the idea concerning it which obtains in the world. So far from being merely a native ability, it is no less than the Spirit of God doing something and using the individual as His instrument in the accomplishment of it. It is distinctly the Spirit's undertaking, and therefore partakes of that supernatural and limitless resource which belongs to the Holy Spirit of God. Thus two important facts are disclosed: the gift is appointed and bestowed by the ascended Christ in glory, and it is wrought by the descended Spirit on the earth; for we read in verse 8, "Wherefore he saith, When he ascended up on high, he led captivity captive, and gave gifts unto men." This is quoted from Psalm 68:18, and the glorified Christ is presented as the One Who, at His ascension, *"received* gifts for men." The gifts were by Him *taken* that they might, in turn, by Him be *given*. In fact the very men for whom the gifts were received and to whom they are given are themselves gifts from the Father to the Son (John 17:2, 6, 9, 11, 12, 24), as the Son is Himself a gift from the Father to men (John 3:16). That it is declared in Psalm 68:18 that Christ *received* gifts, and in Ephesians it is declared that He *gave* gifts, indicates that the *receiving* is unto the *giving*, and that, when applying a previous revelation to a new dispensation, the Spirit is free to vary or qualify the original declaration as He will. Much, indeed, was given to Christ both at the resurrection and the incarnation (Eph. 1:20-23; Phil. 2:9, 11), and what He has received He will yet share with all who are united to Him.

He that ascended (verses 9, 10) is the same also Who first descended to the lower parts of the earth. The undertaking is as much one achievement as it is wrought by One in all its parts. His descent is to lower regions than heaven, yea, even to the grave itself; and His ascent is to a position "far above all heavens." Previously (1:21) He has been seen in a glory incomparable to principalities and powers; but here He is seen, in the living majesty of His own Person, rising to the highest heaven in the exaltation which belongs to the Creator alone. The magnitude of His condescension and all it accomplished, with the surpassing glory of His exaltation and all that it secures for His redeemed, are both alike passed over in the one purpose to identify this adorable and ever blessed Lord as the Bestower of gifts.

Four gifts are here declared (verse 11). Some gifts are divine enablements bestowed upon men (*cf.* Rom. 12:6-8), while others assume the more tangible form of gifted men bestowed upon the Church as a whole.

Apostles

The apostle is the envoy or immediate delegate with the highest authority from the Savior. The term is applied to our Lord Himself (Heb. 3:1), to the Twelve, to Paul, to Barnabas, and to Matthias. Apostles were chosen by Christ or by the Holy Spirit directly and were heralds of the truth of God under divinely provided credentials. They will yet judge the twelve tribes of Israel in the coming Kingdom (Matt. 19:28). Membership in the company of the apostles was conditioned not only upon divine appointment, but upon having been an eyewitness to the resurrected Christ (Acts 1:21). By this credential Paul established and defended his apostleship (1 Cor. 9:1).

Prophets

A prophet of the New Testament order (cf. 2:20 and 3:5) is defined in 1 Corinthians 14:3 as one who "speaketh unto men to edification, to exhortation and comfort." Beyond this illuminating declaration no explanation is needed. The message of the New Testament prophet is more one of *forthtelling* than of *foretelling*. He declares the message of God with exhortation and unto edification and comfort. In the higher meaning of the word, the prophet may be said, along with the apostle, to have ceased with the first generation of the Church; but in a secondary sense, as indicated above, he may be regarded as ministering still.

Evangelists

The evangelist, like the apostle, is unknown in previous dispensations. While the apostle's ministry is evidently limited to the first generation of the Christian era, and while he is given the highest authority to speak as one who has seen the risen Christ, the evangelist's ministry continues throughout the age; and to him is committed the evangel which is God's present and incomparable message of saving grace to all who will believe on Christ. The present peculiar conception of the evangelist as a revivalist and promoter of religious interest within the organized church is hardly the evangelist of the New Testament. Probably the foreign missionary or frontier preacher who enters into hitherto unevangelized fields is more the divine conception of the evangelist. Timothy was charged by the Apostle Paul to do the work of an evangelist (2 Tim. 4:5); namely, to proclaim the glorious evangel to those who are lost.

Pastors and teachers

The omission of the word *some* before the word *teacher* would imply that the ministry of the pastor and that of the teacher are, in the divine economy, committed to one and the same person; and it is well that it is so. In His great grace, God has provided for the comforting and guiding of His people through the ministry of the pastor and for their edification in the sanctifying Scriptures through the ministry of the teacher.

How important it is, then, that the prophet, the evangelist, and the pastor and teacher shall be fully trained for the great task committed to them; for not only do these men serve God in the direct proclamation of the Truth committed to them, but they are (and particularly the pastor and teacher) appointed to leadership in the Church of Christ. This truth, the importance of which can hardly be estimated, is declared in verse 12; for we read that these ministry gifts are "For the perfecting of the saints, for the work of the ministry, for the edifying of the body of Christ." Too often it is supposed from this Scripture that three things are here set forth as descriptive of the detailed duties of those pastors and teachers who are God's gift to the Church. However, the passage assigns to these men the responsibility of "perfecting the saints"; that is, with the view to the equipment of the saints for *their* work of the ministry. The word here translated *perfecting* is a noun which is but once used in the New Testament, and it signifies that *equipment* which all saints should have in their witness and service for Christ. The verb form of the word is found elsewhere (Matt. 4:21, *mending* nets; and Gal. 6:1, where, as a dislocated joint, the unspiritual believer is to be *restored* by one who is spiritual. *Cf.* 2 Cor. 13:11; Heb. 13:21; 1 Peter 5:10).

In view of the New Testament commission in which *all* believers are directed into a vital witnessing for Christ (Matt. 28:19, 20; Mark 16:15; John 17:18; Acts 1:8; 2 Cor. 5:18-20), there is no strange message introduced here with reference to the fact that the saints have a great service to perform. The new truth which is introduced at this point is that the saints are to be *equipped* unto this ministry by the gifted men who are divinely appointed to this task. Thus it is ordained of God that the greatest service is to be wrought by the saints; but it is also recognized that the saints are to be specifically trained for their task. This is the original and never-to-be-improved evangelism of the Church. The multiplied ministries of Sunday School teachers, mission workers, and soul-winners should be not only under the direction of God's appointed leaders, but should be rendered true and effective by faithful instruction.

Indeed, the gifted men must themselves be trained for their tasks and, under modern arrangements, such training is supposed to be provided by the theological seminary. There is needed, likewise, those who, under God, are able to train the gifted men. Probably no greater responsibility could be committed to any man than that he should mould the ideals of the gifted men who, in turn, are to mould the ideals of the whole company of the saints. In this light of this sequence in responsibility, it can be declared that no man, who has not a burning passion for lost men and who is not himself an example of tireless soul-winning zeal, is fitted to serve in a seminary as a fountain source from which these streams of effective ministry flow; for the saints will be what their pastors and teachers equip them to be, and the pastor and teacher will be, to a large degree, what his seminary professor equips him to be.

This order and ministry is unto a divinely appointed consummation (verse 13). It is to go on "till we all come in the unity of the faith, and of the knowledge of the Son of God, unto a perfect man, unto the measure of the stature of the fulness of Christ." There is no thought here of perfecting individual men; it is rather the completion of that body—the Church—which must attain to the measure of the stature of the fulness of Christ. Reference has been made in 2:15 to this great divine consummation, and again it is declared in Romans 11:25 that the present age-long blindness which has come upon Israel will continue "until the fulness of the Gentiles be come in." The Apostle has likewise declared that the Church, which is Christ's body, is "the fulness of him that filleth all in all" (1:23).

It is not the purpose of God that the saints shall be so neglected as to vital truth and so unguided as to leadership in service, that they as mere children are to be "tossed to and fro, and carried about with every wind of doctrine, by the sleight of men, and cunning craftiness, whereby they lie in wait to deceive" (verse 14); but according to the divine plan they are, while speaking the truth in love, to "grow up into him [probably *unto* Him as the Pattern] in all things, which is the head, even Christ" (verse 15); not merely *veracity*, as in verse 25, but a faithful declaration of the message which is divinely committed to them, which message must, if to be effective, be spoken in love.

Sad, indeed, has been the result when the truth has been spoken without love!

The continued emphasis in the New Testament on the importance of advancement in the knowledge of Christ, of growing in grace, of becoming an unashamed workman through the study of the Word, and of a tireless striving for full maturity, should not be unnoticed and unheeded. Likewise, it is true that the Church has lost her testimony and effectiveness in so far as she has turned from these vital, divine injunctions to the substitutes and deceptions which are offered by men. There need be no fear of the ravages of false teachers or their teachings where God's ordained program for His equipped Church has been executed. God alone must be the Judge of those who, sitting in the seat of authority and charged with the purity of doctrinal streams which alone lead to established Christian character and effective service, have allowed the Church to reach her present state of ineffectiveness as a witnessing, soul-winning company.

In the service committed to them, the whole company of believers is likened by the Apostle (verse 16) to a growing body in which each and every part is active in its effort to build up the whole unto maturity. Thus *increase* in the body is secured. Christ is the Source from Whom every vital increase must be derived. He it is Who has undertaken not only to build His Church (Matt. 16:18) by calling out the elect company, but He must, as well, perfect both the individual believer and the corporate body itself.

From the beginning it has pleased God to use the members of Christ's body for the salvation of men, lacking though they often are in educational standing and leadership. Perhaps there is no more suggestive recognition of this self-building character of the Church which is Christ's body than that disclosed in Revelation 19:7, where we read, "Let us be glad and rejoice and give honor to him; for the marriage of the Lamb is come, and his wife hath made herself ready." This original divinely given program of personal evangelism is the method by which the early Church gained the triumph over the forces of the world, and by that same method she might have continued to triumph to this present hour.

Section Thirteen

Ephesians 4:17 to 5:14

17 This I say therefore, and testify in the Lord, that ye henceforth walk not as other Gentiles walk, in the vanity of their mind,

18 Having the understanding darkened, being alienated from the life of God through the ignorance that is in them, because of the blindness of their heart:

19 Who being past feeling have given themselves over unto lasciviousness, to work all uncleanness with greediness.

20 But ye have not so learned Christ;

21 If so be that ye have heard him, and have been taught by him, as the truth is in Jesus:

22 That ye put off concerning the former conversation the old man, which is corrupt according to the deceitful lusts;

23 And be renewed in the spirit of your mind;

24 And that ye put on the new man, which after God is created in righteousness and true holiness.

25 Wherefore putting away lying, speak every man truth with his neighbor: for we are members one of another.

26 Be ye angry, and sin not: let not the sun go down upon your wrath:

27 Neither give place to the devil.

28 Let him that stole, steal no more: but rather let him labor, working with his hands the thing which is good, that he may have to give to him that needeth.

29 Let no corrupt communication proceed out of your mouth, but that which is good to the use of edifying, that it may minister grace unto the hearers.

30 And grieve not the Holy Spirit of God, whereby ye are sealed unto the day of redemption.

31 Let all bitterness, and wrath, and anger, and clamor, and evil speaking, be put away from you, with all malice:

32 And be ye kind one to another, tenderhearted, forgiving one another, even as God for Christ's sake hath forgiven you.

1 Be ye therefore followers of God, as dear children;

2 And walk in love, as Christ also hath loved us, and hath given himself for us an offering and a sacrifice to God for a sweet-smelling savor.

3 But fornication, and all uncleanness, or covetousness, let it not be once named among you, as becometh saints;

4 Neither filthiness, nor foolish talking, nor jesting, which are not convenient: but rather giving of thanks.

5 For this ye know, that no whoremonger, nor unclean person, nor covetous man, who is an idolater, hath any inheritance in the kingdom of Christ and of God.

6 Let no man deceive you with vain words: for because of these things cometh the wrath of God upon the children of disobedience.

7 Be not ye therefore partakers with them.

8 For ye were sometimes darkness, but now are ye light in the Lord: walk as children of light:

9 (For the fruit of the Spirit is in all goodness and righteousness and truth;)

10 Proving what is acceptable unto the Lord.

11 And have no fellowship with the unfruitful works of darkness, but rather reprove them.

12 For it is a shame even to speak of those things which are done of them in secret.

13 But all things that are reproved are made manifest by the light: for whatsoever doth make manifest is light.

14 Wherefore he saith, Awake thou that sleepest, and arise from the dead, and Christ shall give thee light.

Having digressed from the opening theme of the chapter (4:1-3), that he might unfold first, the unifying agencies in the Church which is Christ's body (verses 4-6); second, the diversity of gifts for service (verses 7-11); and third, the fact, motive and purpose of the ministry of the redeemed (verses 12-16), the Apostle now returns (verse 17) to the theme of the consistent walk which should characterize the life of all who are saved. He states emphatically that they should "henceforth walk not as other Gentiles walk, in the vanity of their mind." The correct reading is not *other* Gentiles, which would imply that the saints at Ephesus were also Gentiles. Being saved they were no longer thus to be classed as Gentiles any more than those who were saved from among the Jews were to be classed as Jews. All who are saved have come upon new ground where there is neither Jew nor Gentile, but where "Christ is all, and in all" (Col. 3:11).

A New Relationship

This important implication as to the new relation of the saints to God should be carefully considered. The Gentile estate has been described twice before (2:1-3, 11), and here in Chapter four that estate is said to be "in the vanity [emptiness] of their mind, having the understanding darkened (*cf.* 2 Cor. 4:3, 4; John 3:19), being alienated from the life of God through the ignorance that is in them, because of the blindness [hardness] of their heart" (verses 17, 18). Doubtless the reference to *alienation* is that of the whole race in the Adamic fall. Concerning this Gentile estate it is yet added, "who being past feeling have given themselves over unto lasciviousness, to work all uncleanness with greediness" (verse 19). A very strong metaphor is used in the words *past feeling* since the thought is that of reaching the point in mortification where pain ceases. Similarly, the term *lasciviousness* is wider in its import than fleshly impurity: it is wantonness and rebellion against all divine authority and truth. And, again, both *uncleanness* and *greediness* are to be broadened in their meaning: in the first instance, to impurity of the heart and motive, and in the second instance, to covetousness or lust which knows no restraint in its selfish desires. This description of the moral debauchery of the Gentiles at the time this Epistle was written is, according to what may be known from contemporary history, in no way overdrawn. Such is the universal character of the fallen nature of man. From such moral corruption the Ephesian believers had been saved. Though restrained, indeed, to some extent, by the civilizing influence of the more general knowledge of God and His Truth, the underlying fact of a sin-nature abides unchanged, regardless of its varied manifestations, from the fall of Adam to the present hour.

It is fitting then, in view of the evil from which they have been saved, that these saints be reminded that they "have not so learned Christ" (verse 20); for having come to Him, and having *heard* Him, and having been *taught* by Him as the truth is in Jesus (verse 21) in common with all who believe, they are now called to represent the purity and virtues of Christ (1 Peter 2:9). The change that has been wrought in them—not by mere reformation, but by divine transformation—is no less than that the former manner of life, which has been so vividly described, and the *old man*, which is corrupt according to the deceitful lusts, "is put off." That this is not a command for these saints to do something which was not yet accomplished is seen when two other passages are examined along with this. In Romans 6:6 the *old man* is declared to be crucified in the crucifixion of Christ; and in Colossians 3:9, it is stated of the believers that "ye have put off the old man and his deeds."

The disposing of the *old man* is wrought in that particular aspect of the death of Christ which is *unto sin* (Rom. 6:10), and is also made an *actuality* by the Holy Spirit in all who believe. It should be observed, however, that the *old man* now "put off" is not identical with the *flesh* which, without question, is to abide with each believer to the end of his earthly pilgrimage (Gal. 5:16, 17); but it is rather the first Adamic-relationship which, for the believer, passed out of existence with the death of Christ, being replaced by the New-Creation relationship in Christ, the Last Adam. The connection with the first Adam, which was as vital as the life stream itself, has been broken by divine power to the end that a new connection might be established with Christ.

The appeal here is in accordance with the injunctions of grace. It is because the old man *had been* put off that they were to abstain from their former evil ways, rather than that by abstaining from evil ways the old man *might* be put off. Indeed a renewing of mind by the Holy Spirit is needed (verse 23) to the end that the vital importance of this purity of life shall be comprehended at all times and under all circumstances.

Similarly, they had been taught as the truth is in Christ that they had also "put on the new man, which after God is created in righteousness and true holiness" (verse 24). The *new man* is that which is wrought by the regenerating power of the Spirit—"a new creature" (2 Cor. 5:17; Gal. 6:15)—and, being born of God, cannot participate in the former evil which is the tendency of the flesh and which was the practice of the *old man*. The *new man*, being thus begotten of God, is said to be "created in righteousness and true holiness." The righteousness referred to is that imputed righteousness which Christ is and which He is *made* to those who believe (2 Cor. 5:21), and, likewise, *true* holiness is theirs on the ground of their new position in Christ (Heb. 10:14).

Sins to Avoid

There follows at this point an enumeration of certain cardinal sins which are to be avoided and which would be inconsistent in the lives of those who have put off the *old man* and have put on the *new*. Little need be added here to the list of these sins or the divine exhortations which accompany them.

"Wherefore putting away lying, speak every man truth with his neighbor: for we are members one of another" (verse 25). The "wherefore" with which this plain injunction is introduced relates this and the following injunctions—many indeed, which occupy almost the entire text that remains of this Epistle—to all that has gone before. The appeal is most practical and reasonable in view of the fact that these believers were of one body and fellowship in the Lord.

"Be ye angry, and sin not: let not the sun go down upon your wrath: neither give place to the devil. Let him that stole steal no more: but rather let him labor, working with his hands the thing which is good, that he may have to give to him that needeth" (verses 26-28). By this statement, light is thrown on the question as to what is the true motive for labor and thrift: it is, "that he may have to give to him that needeth." There is no recognition to be allowed among believers of that world-principle which ministers to self or that seeks material things for the mere gratification of desire and possession.

"Let no corrupt communication proceed out of your mouth, but that which is good to the use of edifying, that it may minister grace unto the hearers" (verse 29). Of all the manifestations of the flesh, none is more unfettered than is the liberty of speech;

but this must be restrained in the child of God. Words which do not edify are quite sure to injure, and things which cannot be said confidently in His presence are unfit for the hearing of others. It should be remembered that the flesh is always *contrary* to the Spirit and that it will yield to no other power than the power of God (Gal. 5:16, 17).

Because of the fact that the flesh and the Spirit are contrary the one to the other, the Apostle goes on to say: "and grieve not the Holy Spirit of God, whereby ye are sealed unto the day of redemption" (verse 30). This important text, in addition to its clear implications as to the personality of the Holy Spirit, discloses the engaging fact that the child of God from the moment he is saved is so related to the indwelling Spirit that the sensitiveness of the Spirit supplements the normal functions of conscience. The Christian no longer lives according to his conscience alone, which conscience may be perverted and seared, but with the Holy Spirit Who may be grieved or not grieved by an act, a word, or a thought. That this new standard which the presence of the Spirit creates is higher than the old, and that under these conditions the true believer cannot walk as he walked before, needs no added emphasis (*cf.* Rom. 9:1). So, also, it should be observed that the Spirit Himself indwelling the believer becomes that *sealing* of God which is unto the day of redemption. That "day," be it said, is not the day of our death: it is rather the Day of Christ—the day when the body will be raised, redeemed, and reunited to the glorified soul and spirit. It is the day of "our gathering together unto Him" (2 Thess. 2:1). Thus, as we grieve the Spirit by turning to seek our consolation in the world and not in Christ, so, contrariwise, we satisfy the Spirit when we live wholly unto Christ and look steadfastly for the day of redemption which ever draweth nigh.

The child of God is enjoined to *let* all bitterness, wrath, anger, clamor, evil speaking and malice be put away (verse 31). This can be done only by the power of the Spirit; hence the import of the word *let*, which indicates the extent and direction of the believer's responsibility in the conflict with sin—a conflict, indeed, which may be even unto blood (Heb. 12:4).

Virtues to Put On

As definitely, too, as the evil is to be dismissed, that which is

Christ-like is to take its place, and the same divine power which can disannul the evil can also energize unto the good. We read, "And be ye kind one to another, tenderhearted, forgiving one another, even as God for Christ's sake hath forgive you" (verse 32). The reason for Christian forgiveness, the one toward another, is here seen to be a reversal of the meritorious law-system (cf. Matt. 6:14, 15) and to be an appeal on the ground of super-abounding grace.

Having thus mentioned a fresh evidence of the knowledge-surpassing goodness of Christ, the Apostle resumes his appeal for the Christ-honoring life, contrasting again the former estate of these believers with the present blessings in Christ into which they have been brought through divine grace. The Epistle to the Hebrews is characterized by contrasts which are drawn between the features of the Mosaic order and those of Christianity, while the Epistle to the Ephesians is characterized by its contrasts between the estate of the lost and the estate of the saved.

The fifth Chapter opens with two verses of counsel concerning those characteristics which pertain to a holy life, and these are followed by three verses of counsel concerning those features of corruption which pertain to the flesh. Again, but little comment is needed. It should be noted, however (verses 1, 2), that the saints, here addressed as *His dear children*, are to be "followers of God . . . and walk in love, as Christ also hath loved us, and hath given himself for us an offering and a sacrifice to God for a sweetsmelling savor." How exalted indeed this ideal appears in the midst of the recognition of the works of the flesh which are mentioned in this passage! The inherent law which obligates the creature to do and to be all that the Creator designed has ever rested upon all humanity, but there is a specific privilege extended to God's dear children to follow Him according to the pattern which Christ is and to realize this holy privilege through the divinely provided enablement of the Spirit.

"But fornication, and all uncleanness, or covetousness, let it not be once named among you, as becometh saints; neither filthiness, nor foolish talking, nor jesting, which are not convenient: but rather giving of thanks. For this ye know, that no whoremonger, nor unclean person, nor covetous man, who is an idolater, hath any inheritance in the kingdom of Christ and of God" (verses 3-5).

A distinction is demanded between that lawless sinning of the unregenerate, because of which they are characterized by these unholy designations, and the sinning of the child of God who, being overtaken in a fault or open sin, has descended temporarily to the level of those who habitually practice these evils. This distinction is set forth by the Apostle John in 1 John 3:4-10, and there it will be observed that this form of sin which is *lawlessness* is declared to be no longer possible to the regenerate soul. The Apostle does not teach that Christians do not sin. He rather teaches that they cannot sin *lawlessly* since there is ever in them the divine presence Who not only restrains but Who, in case the believer sins, creates that agony of soul which is described by the Apostle Paul as that of a "wretched man" (Rom. 7:24), and by David as the *aching* of his bones when his spiritual moisture was turned into the drought of summer (Psalm 32:3, 4). Thus the believer who sins even to the terrible length indicated above is not to be classified as an unregenerate sinner. For, though the evil character of the sin is in no way lessened by the fact that a saint commits it, he is not when thus sinning an *habitual* or *lawless* sinner, as the agony of his soul will fully prove (*cf.* 1 John 3:10).

Difference Between Dark and Light

It is distinctly declared (verse 6) that while such deep sin will grieve the Spirit of God, it is these sins in their lawless character which cause the wrath of God to be upon the children of disobedience, which wrath can never come upon the child of God (Rom. 8:1, *R. V.* On the all-inclusiveness of the term *children of disobedience*, see previous notes on Eph. 2:2). The child of God must *not* be a partaker with the lawless sinner, nor indulge in his sins (verse 7). In emphasizing this solemn admonition, the Apostle again reminds these saints of the estate from which they were saved and points out the blessing into which they have come by sovereign grace (verse 8). Being *"light in the Lord"* they are to be as children of the light, or as those who are the product of the light. This strong contrast between darkness and light—terms which are descriptive of the unsaved and saved—is enhanced when it is observed that the unsaved are not here said to be *"in* the dark" but that darkness is in *them,* and that the saved are not merely *in* the light, but the light is in *them.*

The believer may walk in the dark or in the light (1 John 1:5, 6), but that is far different from being darkness, or being light. Certainly the life which is empowered by the Holy Spirit and which hears the fruit of goodness, righteousness and truth is not to be confused with the gross and depraved conduct of the lawless sinner (verse 9). The life energized to holy living is "acceptable unto the Lord" (verse 10) and becomes the ideal ever before the mind of those who are saved. The unfruitful works of darkness are to be reproved and the shame of them is ever to be recognized. Of these works of darkness the believer is not even to speak (verses 11, 12). It is the power of light to make manifest and thereby to reprove (verse 13).

This principle is peculiarly Christian in its character. God does not appoint His witnesses to a ministry of mere contradiction of the evil ideals, practices, or philosophies of the world: He rather directs His ministers to "preach the word" (2 Tim. 4:2), and as witnesses to "hold forth the word of life" (Phil. 2:16) against which nothing that pertains to the darkness can stand. Darkness cannot be dispelled by argument or denunciation: it is dispelled by the outshining of the light.

This section closes with an appeal (verse 14) to those in darkness and death, as indeed all were before the Light of Life came upon them. God it is Who calls whom He will to awake from the sleep of spiritual death.

Section Fourteen

Ephesians 5:15-33

15 See then that ye walk circumspectly, not as fools, but as wise,

16 Redeeming the time, because the days are evil.

17 Wherefore be ye not unwise, but understanding what the will of the Lord is.

18 And be not drunk with wine, wherein is excess; but be filled with the Spirit;

19 Speaking to yourselves in psalms and hymns and spiritual songs, singing and making melody in your heart to the Lord;

20 Giving thanks always for all things unto God and the Father in the name of our Lord Jesus Christ;

21 Submitting yourselves one to another in the fear of God.

22 Wives, submit yourselves unto your own husbands, as unto the Lord.

23 For the husband is the head of the wife, even as Christ is the head of the church: and he is the savior of the body.

24 Therefore as the church is subject unto Christ, let the wives be to their own husbands in every thing.

25 Husbands, love your wives, even as Christ also loved the church, and gave himself for it;

26 That he might sanctify and cleanse it with the washing of water by the word,

27 That he might present it to himself a glorious church, not having spot, or wrinkle, or any such thing; but that it should be holy and without blemish.

28 So ought men to love their wives as their own bodies. He that loveth his wife loveth himself.

29 For no man ever yet hated his own flesh; but nourisheth and cherisheth it, even as the Lord the church:

30 For we are members of his body, of his flesh, and of his bones,
31 For this cause shall a man leave his father and mother, and shall be joined unto his wife, and they two shall be one flesh.
32 This is a great mystery: but I speak concerning Christ and the church.
33 Nevertheless, let every one of you in particular so love his wife even as himself; and the wife see that she reverence her husband.

As we enter this section of the Epistle it is with a consciousness that the dark picture of the manifestation of the flesh, whether in saint or sinner, has had a faithful portrayal, and that the divinely enabled, God-honoring life is infinitely desirable. The contrast between these two extremes could hardly be drawn by human pen. The Apostle calls again, for the seventh and last time in this Epistle, for a holy walk which is circumspect or punctually accurate in doing in every particular only that which is pleasing to God (verse 15). The extremes of folly and wisdom are here represented. As a child may be guided by the wisdom, experience, and love of the parent, so heavenly wisdom is available to the child of God and the walk, as guided and empowered by the Spirit, will be accurate according to the standards of heavenly holiness. Indeed, the days are evil, all of them (verse 16), and the time—so brief—should be redeemed, or "bought up." The riches of strength and fellowship resulting from the divine Presence will not be experienced apart from certain well-defined concessions; but how little is ever paid in comparison with the treasures secured!

A Circumspect Walk

There is more here than merely a wise choice on the part of those who are willing to make that choice. The *circumspect walk* is distinctly the *will of the Lord* for each and every child of God (verse 17). Therefore, the present walk in the flesh is not only a folly of infinite proportion, but is a distinct *disobedience* and *disregard* of the revealed will of the One Who has saved us at measureless cost. The antinomian deception is that exactness of conduct is an indifferent thing so long as there is soundness of doctrine; but such error is most serious. True piety is not a thoughtless security, but rather a watchful sobriety which is a daily habit of mind. There is marvelous advantage to the one who knows the doctrines and stands secure in their glorious fulness; but there is need, as well, that the doctrine shall be adorned (Tit. 2:10).

At this point there is perplexity created sooner or later in every sincere believer's mind. He has to some degree recognized the necessity and reasonableness of the circumspect life; but, like the Apostle of old, he has been forced to cry, "*how* to perform that which is good I find not" (Rom. 7:18). High and holy ideals which are not attained only tend to the most distressing spiritual discomfort. Such, indeed, is a "wretched man" (Rom. 7:24). With the mind he serves the law of God, but with the flesh the law of sin (Rom. 7:25). Vain has been the effort of saints to crucify the flesh with its affections and lusts. Even the regenerate *self* cannot control the mind of the flesh. Help must come from God and this He has provided, but not according to the reasonings of men. Turning to the Scriptures, we discover that the "old man" *was* crucified with Christ (Rom. 6:5, *R.V.*), and that they that are Christ's *have* crucified the flesh with the affections and lusts (Gal. 5:24); not *some* of those who are Christ's, but *all*. Such truth can mean nothing less than that the *old* man and the *flesh* were divinely judged in the death of Christ. He died as much *unto* sin (the sin-nature, *cf.* Rom. 6:10) as He died *for* our sins; the latter making *justification* a possibility, and the former making *sanctification of life* a possibility. The latter is the ground on which the Spirit is free to *regenerate* those who believe in Christ, and the former is the ground on which the Spirit is free to *deliver* those believers who yield themselves to God and walk by means of, and in dependence on, the Spirit.

The problem then is not one of *self-crucifixion*, as direct and practical as that seems to be; but it is rather that of trusting One Who is able to give moment-by-moment deliverance on the ground of the fact that the *old man* and the *flesh* are both alike already judged in the crucifixion of Christ. The two propositions—one of self-crucifixion, the other of victory by the overcoming power of the Spirit and on the ground of Christ's crucifixion—are principles of action as far removed from each other as the east is removed from the west; and one is ever and always a failure because of the impotency of man, while the other, when fully appropriated, is ever and always a success, being ordained of God and sustained by His infinite strength.

Being Filled with the Spirit

It is not strange, then, that when turning to a fuller recognition of the heavenly virtues which the believer is called to manifest, the Apostle should press an unqualified command, namely to be *filled with the Spirit* (verse 18). To be sure, there is a feeble stimulant to the flesh in wine which, however, only leads to riot of mind and action; but over against the stimulant to the flesh there is an abundant enabling power available from the Spirit which leads to all those graces which are none other than the life which is *Christ* (Gal. 2:20; 5:22, 23). It is significant that, in the New Testament, wine is thrice held over against the Spirit-filled life (*cf.* Luke 1:15; Acts 2:12-17), as its opposite or counterfeit.

The command to be Spirit-filled is imperative, both as a divine necessity and as a divine authority. There is nothing optional on the human side. However, the tense of the verb is significant indicating, as it does, not a once-for-all *crisis*-experience, but rather a constant infilling. The New Testament teaches that all believers are *indwelt* by the Spirit of God (John 7:37-39; Rom. 5:5; 8:9; 1 Cor. 2:12; 6:19), but it also teaches that those in whom the Spirit abides need always to be *getting filled* with the Spirit.

The Spirit's filling is more, then, than His abiding Presence; it is His activities realized. To be filled with the Spirit is to have the Spirit fulfilling in us all that He came into our hearts to do. Again, to be getting filled with the Spirit is not to receive more of the Spirit; it is rather that more *conformity* to His mind and will is accorded to Him by the one in whom He already abides. The Spirit is *received* at the moment one believes on Christ for salvation (John 7:37-39), but the believer is *filled* with the Spirit only at such a time in which he does not grieve the Spirit by unconfessed sin (Eph. 4:32), nor resist the Spirit by unwillingness to do His will (1 Thess. 5:19), and when the heart of such an one exercises that constant dependence upon the Spirit which is elsewhere termed, *walking by means of the Spirit* (Gal. 5:16; Rom. 8:4).

Blessed, indeed, are the provisions of God which do not leave the child of God in uncertainty as to what the Spirit will do when He fills the life and heart. How uncertain all understanding of the Spirit-filled life would be if the identification of the precise character of the work of the Spirit were limited to the evidence each believer might gain through experience. The Spirit's work is to produce Christian character (Gal. 5:22, 23), Christian service by the exercise of a gift (1 Cor. 12:4-7), knowledge of the Scriptures through the teaching ministry of the Spirit (John 16:12-15; *cf.* Rom. 8:14, 16, 26, 27; 1 John 2:27); but in this context it has pleased the Spirit to mention only the fact that the Spirit-filled life is one of ceaseless *praise* and *gratitude* (verses 19, 20).

All manifestations of divine power in the heart are in the line of things most vital and are so practical that any child of God will detect the presence or absence of them in his own heart. It is only by a supernatural power that one may always be *singing* and giving thanks *always* for *all* things. There is no reference in this passage to the *baptism with the Spirit,* by which believers are joined to the Lord as members in one body (1 Cor. 12:15); the Spirit's filling, it will be observed, results rather in those inner graces and those outward manifestations in service which are the outliving of the indwelling Christ.

A Call to Submission

Beginning with verse 21, the important duty of Christian submission is presented with those truths which are related to it. Wives are to be subject to husbands, children to parents, and servants to masters. The submission of the wife to the husband is placed on a very high plane—"as unto the Lord" (verse 22)—and in this relationship, being likened to Christ and the Church which is His body and bride, the wife is ordained of God to be subject to the husband as the Church is subject to Christ (verses 23, 24). This is not difficult for the wife to do providing the husband is unto her as he is enjoined to be in verse 25, where we read that the husband is to love his wife even as Christ also loved the Church and gave Himself for it.

Whatever may be the mind of the modern world regarding the sacred relationship between husbands and wives, the

Christian doctrine is not obscure. Misgoverned affections on the husband's part might unwittingly concede to the wife the ruling place in the home, or her own force of character might assume the place of directing; but it stands unchallenged to the present hour that the highest peace and greatest spiritual blessing result when believing wives and husbands are duly conformed to these plain and wholesome instructions.

Nothing need be said here of the duties falling upon husband or wife when, perchance, the other party in the union is unsaved. The Scripture has elsewhere treated fully such a case (1 Cor. 7:12-17; 1 Pet. 3:1). In this context, however, the wife and husband are viewed as each being alike in Christ. How else could the husband be likened to Christ, or the wife be likened to the Church? The similar injunction to both husbands and wives set forth in Colossians 3:18, 19 may well be quoted here: "Wives, submit yourselves unto your own husbands, as it is fit in the Lord. Husbands, love your wives, and be not bitter against them."

At this point in the theme, the Apostle reverts to the order of truth which characterized the opening portion of this Epistle. The Church alone is in view as the one for whom Christ gave Himself to die upon the Cross. It is true also that His death is provisionally for those even who do not claim its gracious blessing, and that His death is the ground on which God will yet do for Israel what He is now doing for the Church (for God will bring that nation into a place of right relation to Himself and purify her dross—Ezek. 16:20-63; 36:25-29; Isa. 1:25); but the fact of His death for the Church is here given the place of supreme importance. Certainly Jehovah's love for Israel could not be doubted (Jer. 31:22), but the fact that these two great divine purposes—that of Israel's earthly blessing, and that of the out-calling of the Church—have so much in common is no argument that these purposes unite in one divine purpose in the past, now, or ever. It is to be expected that Israel's portion would be proclaimed in those Old Testament Scriptures which are addressed to her; while the portion for the Church will be found in the Epistles of the New Testament. The heavenly blessings which belong to the Church, it will be observed, constitute the message of this section of this Epistle.

A Plan for the Church

In verses 25-27, the past, present, and future of the Church are revealed: (1) "Christ also loved the church and gave himself for it" (2) "that he might sanctify and cleanse it with the washing of water by the word," and (3) "that he might present it to himself a glorious church, not having spot, or wrinkle, or any such thing; but that it should be holy and without blemish." No such purpose has been revealed for any other people than the Church as is here described. Though God included Israel in His redemptive purposes and will yet purify her, it is never said that He will present Israel to Himself glorified, not having spot or wrinkle, and holy, and without blemish. Of the Church it is said that each and every member of that glorious company will be conformed to His image, and when those who are His own see Him, they will be like Him. The marvelous heavenly perfections which are determined for the Church in glory could be no less than this, in view of the position and place she is to occupy in that coming glory. Unto her it is given to be forever glorified together with Him (Col. 3:4), to go wherever He goes, and to reign with Him upon His throne. Nothing but divine transformation reaching to the last detail of perfection in each individual could so consummate this heavenly purpose; and such is Christ's past, present, and future ministry to the Church.

Reverting now (verse 28) to the subject from which attention has been drawn but for a moment, the message continues, "So ought men to love their wives as their own bodies. He that loveth his wife loveth himself. For no man ever yet hated his own flesh; but nourisheth and cherisheth it, even as the Lord the church: for we are members of his body, of his flesh, and of his bones" (verses 29, 30).

Of the seven figures used in the New Testament to set forth the relationship which exists between Christ and the Church, two appear in this context, and in each of these Christ's headship is declared. In the former, the Church is seen to be that body of which He is the Head; in the latter, the Church is seen as the Bride, and, as the Bridegroom, Christ is her Head. It is the Bridegroom headship over the Church which establishes the fact that the husband is head over the wife (Eph. 1:22; 4:15; 5:23; Col. 1:18; 1 Cor. 11:3). There are far-reaching implications under each of these figures as to the authority which is Christ's over those who are His own—an authority absolute and final, yet softened by an immeasurable knowledge-surpassing love (3:18, 19).

With an evident backward look to Genesis 2:24 and in view of the infinite love of Christ for the Church, the Apostle states, "For this cause shall a man leave his father and mother, and shall be joined unto his wife, and they two shall be one flesh" (verse 31). "This is a great mystery" (sacred secret). It is a mystery which draws into itself all those marvelous hidden meanings that exist in the eternal union which is now being formed, and is yet to be consummated in the glory, between the heavenly Bridegroom and His perfected and glorified Bride (verse 32).

The reference in verse 31 to the declaration found in Genesis 2:23, 24 determines the important fact that this context (verses 21-33) refers not primarily to the figure of the Church as the body with Christ as her Head, but rather to the headship of Christ as Bridegroom over the Bride; thus refuting the erroneous claim that Israel, and not the Church, is the Bride of Christ. It is true that Israel is the repudiated, apostate wife of Jehovah yet to be forgiven, purified, and restored (Jer. 3:1, 14, 20; Ezek. 16:1-54). But such an idea is far removed from the thought of a "chaste virgin" espoused, but not yet married, to the Son of God. Likewise, it is untenable to claim that the earthly people—Israel—will be caught away from the earth into heaven and there appear at the marriage of the Lamb as the Lamb's wife amid those scenes of surpassing glory (Rev. 19:7). That glory belongs to the Church which company He is perfecting to a degree that will qualify her for His eternal companionship in heaven (Rom. 8:29; 1 John 3:3).

This whole context which presents so much truth concerning the relation that exists between Christ and the Church, and that should exist between husbands and wives, closes with the following injunction: "Nevertheless let every one of you in particular so love his wife even as himself; and the wife see that she reverence her husband."

Section Fifteen

Ephesians 6:1-24

1 Children, obey your parents in the Lord: for this is right.

2 Honor thy father and mother; which is the first commandment with promise;

3 That it may be well with thee, and thou mayest live long on the earth.

4 And, ye fathers, provoke not your children to wrath: but bring them up in the nurture and admonition of the Lord.

5 Servants, be obedient to them that are your masters according to the flesh, with fear and trembling, in singleness of your heart, as unto Christ;

6 Not with eyeservice, as menpleasers; but as the servants of Christ, doing the will of God from the heart;

7 With good will doing service, as to the Lord, and not to men:

8 Knowing that whatsoever good thing any man doeth, the same shall he receive of the Lord, whether he be bond or free.

9 And, ye masters, do the same things unto them, forbearing threatening, knowing that your Master also is in heaven; neither is there respect of persons with him.

10 Finally, my brethren, be strong in the Lord, and in the power of his might.

11 Put on the whole armor of God, that ye may be able to stand against the wiles of the devil.

12 For we wrestle not against flesh and blood, but against principalities, against powers, against the rulers of the darkness of this world, against spiritual wickedness in high places.

13 Wherefore take unto you the whole armor of God, that ye may be able to withstand in the evil day, and having done all, to stand.

14 Stand therefore, having your loins girt about with truth, and having on the breastplate of righteousness;

15 And your feet shod with the preparation of the gospel of peace;

16 Above all, taking the shield of faith, wherewith ye shall be able to quench all the fiery darts of the wicked.

17 And take the helmet of salvation, and the sword of the Spirit, which is the word of God:

18 Praying always with all prayer and supplication in the Spirit, and watching thereunto with all perseverance and supplication for all saints;

19 And for me, that utterance may be given unto me, that I may open my mouth boldly, to make known the mystery of the gospel,

20 For which I am an ambassador in bonds; that therein I may speak boldly, as I ought to speak.

21 But that ye also may know my affairs, and how I do, Tychicus, a beloved brother and faithful minister in the Lord, shall make known to you all things:

22 Whom I have sent unto you for the same purpose, that ye might know our affairs, and that he might comfort your hearts.

23 Peace be to the brethren, and love with faith, from God the Father and the Lord Jesus Christ.

24 Grace be with all them that love our Lord Jesus Christ in sincerity. Amen.

The high and holy manner of life which results from the filling of the Spirit is again in view at the opening of Chapter six, and the one theme of *submission* is emphasized. Children are to be obedient to parents, and servants to masters. Similarly, there is a corresponding responsibility pressed upon the parents and the masters as was declared in the preceding injunctions to husbands and wives (5:21-33). It is to be observed, however, that a different Greek word is used to indicate the obedience of the wife than is used to indicate the obedience of the children and servants—a word which recognizes a more equal and mature responsibility each to the other on the part of the husband and wife.

The counsel given to children to obey their parents (6:1-3) is followed by an injunction to fathers (rendered *parents* with equal propriety) to "provoke not your children to wrath: but bring them up in the nurture and admonition of the Lord" (verse 4). *Nurture* is *discipline*, and *admonition* is faithful *warning* as to the perils of evil conduct. It will be seen; however, that this instruction to parents (*cf.* Col. 3:21) is not included in the instruction contained in the decalogue. Grace obligations *"in the Lord"* are mutual in character, not only between husbands and wives, parents and children, masters and servants, but between the Father of mercies and the child He has redeemed out of bondage.

Children and Parents

The importance of implicit obedience on the part of the children, though little heeded today, is nevertheless greatly stressed in the Scriptures and on the ground that it is *right;* which indeed it is, and from every point of consideration. Obedience on the part of children is included as one of the commandments of the decalogue. As a child, Christ was an example of perfect obedience (Luke 2:51); and the opposite, or disobedience to parents, is set forth as one of the most serious of evils which characterize the repulsive degradation of the heathen (Rom. 1:30); and the apostasy of the last days (2 Tim. 3:2). Instruction concerning relationship between parents and children, being restricted to those who are *"in the Lord"* (verse 1), will hardly be heeded by the unregenerate; but how binding it is upon those who are saved! A theory, born of the insufficient ideals of the world, which is to the effect that the will of the child should not be crossed but merely guided, is bearing its fruit today in unprecedented lawlessness and disregard of God. That Christian parents are adopting these modern ideals and, by so much, are disregarding the plain instructions of God's Word, is an error of serious consequences. Where may such a Christian parent expect a child to learn obedience to God if parental discipline has been neglected?

In emphasizing this injunction to children, the Apostle cites the fact that the command for obedience was a major feature of the decalogue and is the one command of the ten which was attended by promise. There is no necessity for the assumption that the Apostle is here *applying* the decalogue to children *in the Lord;* he is rather strengthening his appeal by indicating the universal import of obedience on the part of children as enjoined by God in all human history. The obedient child under the law was promised long life in the land which God had given. The Christian, who is a stranger and pilgrim (1 Pet. 2:11) in this world, neither possesses a land nor is he seeking a long life; to him the days are evil and he awaits the soon coming of his Lord from heaven.

Employers and Employees

The injunction to masters and servants (verses 5-9), here addressed to the slave owner and his slave, is equally applicable to the employer and the employee of these modern times. The Scripture bearing on this particular relationship is extensive (*cf.* Philemon 1-25; Col. 3:22-25; 1 Cor. 7:21, 22; 1 Tim. 6:1, 2; Titus 2:9, 10; 1 Peter 2:18, 19). It will be observed that these injunctions are restricted to those who are *in Christ,* whether masters or servants. Service for Christ is the one matter of concern in either case. The master is reminded of his bond servitude to Christ, and the servant is reminded that he is to recognize his lowly position as being the will of God for him and to be faithful, not merely to secure favor with earthly masters, but as one who is "doing the will of God from the heart." The servant must realize that his state not only could be, but would be, changed were it the will of God, and that until it is changed—if ever—the glorious privilege of doing God's will is to be discovered in the very position of servitude in which he finds himself.

There is precious comfort to be derived from the fact that the highest of all attainments is not the place of freedom from the authority of men or the place of authority over men; it is rather that of *finding* and *doing* the will of God. The heavenly Master is no respecter of persons. The door of opportunity to rise to the sublime heights of doing His will is open no more to earthly masters than it is to earthly servants. Where, indeed, is there any inequality to be observed any longer between a master and his slave if perchance each, by divine grace, is exalted to the place of sonship in the Father's house? Might it not be that the slave, because of his very stress of servitude borne in gracious obedience to Christ, shall in the end secure a far more honorable recognition in the day of Christ than the master who, possessing this world's goods, learned little in the school of suffering?

In Conclusion

Having reached the conclusion of this incomparable letter the Apostle introduces once again the believer's responsibility with the words: "Finally, my brethren, be strong in the Lord, and in the power of his might" (verse 10). Such divine energy, so woefully needed, is provided by the strengthening of the inner man through the Spirit (3:16), and by the filling of the Spirit (5:18). Thus it is seen that this new and effective resource of triumphant deliverance in daily life, and over the world, the flesh, and the devil, is introduced here only as the consummation of all that has gone before.

There should be no uncertainty at this point as to the reality of the conflict—far surpassing human strength—nor of the sufficient ability of the Lord to give triumphant deliverance. The problem is rather one of being in such reasonable relation to Him that every moment shall be radiant with His overcoming power. It is the problem of the justified one going on to "live by faith" (Hab. 2:4; Rom. 1:17; Gal. 3:11; Heb. 10:38). Triumphant conquest upon a principle of *faith* is ever the one responsibility of the believer. A Christian is not appointed to fight his foes single-handedly and alone; he is to fight *"the good fight of faith."* Thus the Apostle could say at the end of his life of wonderful service, "I have fought a good fight" (2 Tim. 4:7); learning, as he had, how to perform that which is good (Rom. 7:18). To be *"strong in the Lord and in the power of his might"* calls for an unceasing dependence upon God, in which dependence all confidence in self is abandoned. The conflict is not a crisis-experience where the deliverance is won in a moment of time forever; it is rather to *walk by means of the Spirit* (Gal. 5:16-18), and there could be no more expressive term employed than to liken this unceasing conflict to a *walk* by means of the Spirit.

Recognizing the Enemy

As every breath exhaled is incipient death, so every step is an incipient fall. The very act of taking a step is that of abandoning one's poise with the confidence that it will be regained by the new step to be taken. Should the expected step fail through tripping, that incipient fall becomes an actual fall. In like manner, the child of God must learn to repose his confidence in the divine power; not once-for-all, but moment-by-moment and unceasingly to the end of his earthly journey. While the conflict is threefold, namely, with the world, the flesh, and the devil, the Apostle presents here only the conflict with the devil. The whole armor of God is to be put on "that he might be able to stand against the strategies of the devil" (verse 11). Two important figures of speech are thus employed: first, *"the whole armor of God,"* which is described later in this context, and second, the phrase *"to stand,"* the full meaning of which is disclosed by the accompanying words, "against the strategies of the devil." In this connection, it is interesting to observe that as pilgrims we *walk*, as witnesses we *go*, as contenders we *run*, and as fighters we *stand*.

How absolute are ideals held before the Christian in this conflict with Satan! The day is evil and the odds against him are overwhelming; yet he is *to stand* (verse 13), but only, indeed, in the power of the Lord and in the strength of His might.

The phrase *wrestling in warfare* suggests hand-to hand combat and is a figure that is not overdrawn. This wrestling is not against mere men of flesh and blood (it should be remarked that the Apostle is not denying at this point the believer's conflict with the flesh and its desires, but is rather asserting that this is no mere human combat), but rather "against principalities, against powers, against the rulers of the darkness of this world, against spiritual wickedness in high places" (verse 12).

As in the case of several passages which convey definite truth relative to the person, power and strategy of Satan, the precise meaning of this verse is obscure through faulty translation. An extended discussion of all the problems of exegesis found in this passage is uncalled for here. However, the force of this important appeal as to victory over this great foe will be found hidden in this one verse.

The War in Heaven

The reader has already been made familiar with the fact that there are vast multitudes of spirit beings (1:21). These are divided into two classes—the fallen, and the unfallen. There are those known as the *holy angels* whose ministries were available to Christ at the time of His death (Matt. 26:53), and there are unnumbered legions of evil spirits who serve the purpose of Satan (Mark 5:9, 15; Luke 8:30). These two hosts will yet wage a war in heaven when the evil spirits under the leadership of Satan will be banished from that realm forever, being expelled by the holy angels under the leadership of Michael (Rev. 12:7-10).

Though the character of those beings designated "principalities and powers" is not always declared to be evil (1:21; Rom. 8:38), in this instance they are evil (*cf.* Col. 2:15). The phrase *"rulers of the darkness of this world"* is better rendered *"the world-rulers of this darkness."* That this age is one of spiritual darkness, apart from the light which God bestows, need not be argued; but it is a most important truth, here stated, that far-reaching authority is vested in these evil spirits. Such authority on the part of evil spirits will not be doubted by those who with reverent hearts discover the testimony of the Scriptures on this extensive theme (*cf.* Matt. 12:26; Luke 4:6; John 14:30; 16:11; 2 Cor. 4:4; Isa. 14:12-17). This conflict is declared to be in the sphere of the *heavenly*, which is the sphere of spiritual associations and realities.

How few of God's children are aroused to this combat! Is it not too often a lost battle when spiritual stress and exercise are in question? Who will not concede that he is often defeated in the ministry of prayer, or in the pursuance of his God-given privilege to witness for Christ? As the "spirit of error," Satan seeks to counteract the testimony of the spirit of truth; while as the "spirit of wickedness," he incites the flesh to protracted rebellion against the holy and ever blessed will of God.

Following this most impressive declaration as to the nature of the conflict and the superior character of the foe both as to numbers and strength, it could not be otherwise than that the Apostle would stress again, as he does (verse 13), the necessity of *standing* against this foe in an *evil* day, and, having done all, *to stand.* So, again, he refers to the armor of God which God has provided for those who wage this battle. Every effort is made by the Apostle through the Spirit to alarm the child of God into recognizing the serious position in which he is placed.

The child of God has died in Christ's death (Col. 3:1-3) and a dead man has no enemies, nor should the *believer* recognize any individuals as *personal* enemies. The enemy with whom the believer is in conflict is such on the ground of the believer's relation to God. The enmity is primarily between Satan and God, and Satan's *fiery darts* are aimed not at the believer alone, as in personal hatred, but at the divine Person Who indwells the believer. We cannot inherit the treasures of the divine Person without inheriting Satan's enmity and hatred toward God. It is well to remember that Satan would strike the child of God even unto death if he were permitted to do so (*cf.* Job 1:1 to 2:10). The recognition of this alarming fact will tend both to cast those that are saved upon God, and to encourage them to render praise to God for His protection, which praise, alas, is too often lacking.

At the opening of verse 14, the Apostle uses the word *stand* for the fourth time in this context. This word is full of most impressive suggestion as to the stability and vigor with which the Christian is expected to confront his mortal enemy. In this combat an armor is provided and is essential beyond estimation. The Greek word is *panoplia* and when used with the word *whole*, as in verse 11, the clear intimation is of the fact that there is nothing omitted from this divinely provided equipment.

Weapons for Warfare

The believer is counted upon to appropriate that provision, apart from which he must so certainly fail. To this end it becomes him to recognize each part of this panoply and to reckon it by faith to be his own. These items are: a girdle, a breastplate, a protection for the feet, a shield, a helmet, and a sword.

The *girdling of the loins* with truth is the necessary binding with that strength which comes only through the knowledge of the truth of God. The *instructed* Christian is girded for battle.

The *breastplate of righteousness* refers to the imputed righteousness of God which is *made* unto us, being *in Christ*. No "rags" of human righteousness will serve as a breastplate in this combat. But what limitless defense is provided, and what confidence of safety is imparted through the conscious recognition of an unalterable possession of an absolutely perfect standing *in Christ!*

The *feet are shod* with the preparation of the Gospel of Peace. This conflict is for those alone who, by grace, are standing in the saving power of Another.

The *shield of faith* is that instrument of conflict which will receive and quench the fiery darts of the wicked one. These darts are directed at the very center of the believer's spiritual life. There is no other provision whereby they may be held in check. God graciously provides the shield, but how serious it is for that exposed warrior who neglects this feature of his equipment!

The *helmet of salvation* might easily include every aspect of saving grace, even that which protects the head and qualifies the mind in the conflict.

The *sword of the Spirit* is the Word of God. It is the Spirit's sword and will be wielded by His strength and skill in the hand of the one who knows that Word and is yielded to God (verses 14 to 17).

The inestimable importance of "praying always with all prayer and supplication in the Spirit, and watching thereunto with all perseverance and supplication for all saints" is the message of verse 18. Again the child of God is depended upon to exercise his will and to elect that place of dependence upon God which is intended both for his own benefit in the battle and for the benefit of all his fellow-warriors for whom he should pray. Thus fully equipped, the child of God, those of us believers who make up the church, can glorify the God whom we serve, the One who has chosen us to live this new life in Him.

The Epistle closes with the personal word of the Apostle—a plea for unabating prayer in his own behalf that he may be faithful, a message about his representative Tychicus whom he sends unto Ephesus, and the benediction: "Peace be to the brethren, and love with faith, from God the Father and the Lord Jesus Christ. Grace be with all them that love our Lord Jesus Christ in sincerity. Amen."

Topical Index

Textual Index